Your Towns and Cities in the

Lancaster
in the Great War

For my beloved wife, Brenda
1942–2008

Your Towns and Cities in the Great War

Lancaster
in the Great War

John Fidler

Pen & Sword
MILITARY

First published in Great Britain in 2016 by
PEN & SWORD MILITARY
an imprint of
Pen and Sword Books Ltd
47 Church Street
Barnsley
South Yorkshire S70 2AS

ISBN 978 1 47384 611 1

A CIP record for this book is available from the British Library

Printed and bound in England
by CPI Group (UK) Ltd, Croydon, CR0 4YY

Typeset in Times New Roman by Chic Graphics

Pen & Sword Books Ltd incorporates the imprints of
Pen & Sword Archaeology, Atlas, Aviation, Battleground, Discovery,
Family History, History, Maritime, Military, Naval, Politics, Railways,
Select, Social History, Transport, True Crime, Claymore Press,
Frontline Books, Leo Cooper, Praetorian Press, Remember When,
Seaforth Publishing and Wharncliffe.

For a complete list of Pen and Sword titles please contact
Pen and Sword Books Limited
47 Church Street, Barnsley, South Yorkshire, S70 2AS, England
E-mail: enquiries@pen-and-sword.co.uk
Website: www.pen-and-sword.co.uk

Contents

Introduction

During the Great War the town (not yet a city) of Lancaster stood on its own: the neighbouring towns of Morecambe and Heysham, and the villages of the Lancaster Rural District were not incorporated until 1974. This book therefore relates to that Lancaster. Similarly, while the local regiment, the King's Own Royal Lancaster Regiment had its depot in the city, its recruiting area was more widespread. When referring to military casualties and honours, I have tried to identify natives of Lancaster and to show examples of the many units and fields in which they served.

Among those who have assisted me in the writing of this book, I must single out Heather Dowler of the City Museum, Andy Henderson and Claire Blundell of Ripley St Thomas CE Academy, Sarah Fisher of Bowerham School, and Rose Welshman of Lancaster Royal Grammar School. I have consulted the admirable website of the Lancaster Military Heritage Group and I am grateful to the staff of Lancaster City Library who have endured my presence day by day at the microfilm reader as I worked through the files of the *Lancaster Guardian* and *Lancaster Observer* for the relevant years.

The cover photograph shows the Lancaster Pals returning from a church parade. (LCM)

CHAPTER 1

Lancaster in 1914

In the summer of 1914 Lancaster, the ancient county town of what is properly the County Palatine of Lancaster, remained essentially the market town which it had been for centuries. Its name betrays its Roman origins (the military camp on the Lune), established to cover the lowest crossing point on the river. The camp, originally a marching camp with a turf wall later rebuilt in stone, had been largely overlaid by the Norman castle and the Priory Church. The Benedictine Priory was originally a daughter church of the Abbey of Seez in Normandy, later of Syon in Middlesex, but after 1430 (a century before the dissolution of the monasteries by Henry VIII and Thomas Cromwell) it ceased to be a monastic foundation and became the parish church of Lancaster. The castle had been a northern bastion against the Scots, who had twice taken and burnt the town. Its last military use was in the civil wars, when it was taken by parliamentary troops in 1643; it was later used as a prison.

Granted a borough charter in 1193 by John, Count of Mortain (soon to become King John), Lancaster had its own council of burgesses, with the right to hold twice weekly markets (still held) and horse fairs twice a year, and it later had the right to send members to parliament. The Assizes were held twice a year and other legal and mercantile services were provided over the years. A river port of significance in the late seventeenth and eighteenth centuries, it had traded with the Baltic for naval stores (timber, turpentine, resin, hemp and flax) for its two shipyards, and been marginally involved in slaving in the 'Africa Trade', by some four to eight ships each year. Its mercantile importance dwindled as the Lune silted up and ships grew larger, but it still had access to the sea from the port of Heysham and, via a connecting branch of the Lancaster Canal, to the little port of Glasson Dock.

The import of mahogany had led to the establishment in 1728 of the cabinet makers Gillow whose fine furniture was not only sold locally, but also exported to the West Indies and Virginia. By the late nineteenth century they had diversified into fitting out town halls and ocean liners with quality panelling; their workshops on St Leonardgate remained in business until 1963, when they had a new lease of life as offices and laboratories for the new University of Lancaster.

The manufacture of cotton was mainly in the hands of the Storey and, later, the Williamson families, who between them employed the bulk of the population in their mills, where the manufacture of cotton had, by 1914, largely given way to linoleum and table baize. The main Storey's mill was at White Cross, of which the principal building is now the Adult Education Centre, surrounded by a small industrial estate. Moor Lane North is now Mill Hall, a student hall of residence, and across the road, Moor Lane South has become a warehouse, initially for Reebok and latterly for the National Health Service. Of the Williamson mills, the Bath and Greenfield Mills have been demolished, to be replaced by housing. The derelict St George's Mill is being demolished, but manufacture still goes on at the extensive Lune mills.

As was usual among industrialists of the time, both families had made provision for the enhancement of the city by providing the Storey Institute and Williamson Park. The former made provision for a library and reading room to improve the education of working men, the latter gave the city leisure facilities by the landscaping of the quarry out of which the houses of the city had been built. It was later given lasting grandeur by the erection of the Ashton Memorial (which Pevsner in the Lancashire volume of his *Buildings of England*, called 'the grandest folly in England') whose baroque architecture and copper dome still dominate the city.

A new town hall and a statue of Queen Victoria were 1909 additions by James Williamson's son (now ennobled as Lord Ashton). With the earlier closure of the Carriage and Wagon Works on Caton Road, the only other manufacturing enterprise of any size was the Phoenix Foundry, appropriately in Phoenix Street. Remarkably, there were no fewer than seven stained glass manufacturers, of which Shrigley and

Storey Institute (LCM)

New Town Hall (LCM)

The Fire Brigade (LCM)

Hunt on Castle Hill and Abbott & Co on Butterfield Street off Damside, were probably the best known. The others were Lambert & Moore at Greaves, Seward & Co in Sun Street; James Holmes on Fenton Street; Barraclough & Sanders on Brunton Road and Eaton & Bulfield on Castle Hill. Another small enterprise was Anthony Bell's marble works on Parliament Street.

Lancaster was a key town on the main road from London to Carlisle (the modern A6), and the Lancaster Canal, linking the town with Kendal opened in 1797. Unfortunately, the expense of Rennie's magnificent Lune aqueduct did not leave enough money for a similar crossing of the Ribble, and the canal remained isolated from the main network. The railway had come early to Lancaster: the Lancaster and Preston Junction Railway opened in 1840, with its terminus at the Penny Street station (now the nurses' home of the Royal Lancaster Infirmary). When the later Lancaster and Carlisle Railway opened its Castle station in 1846, passengers had at first to make an inconvenient transfer by wagonette, but a rail link soon made this unnecessary. The 'little' North Western railway, which had its station at Green Ayre, gave connections to Morecambe and Leeds, with the Morecambe line being electrified in 1908.

There was an ancient grammar school, originating in the thirteenth century, and endowed by a local merchant, John Gardyner of Bailrigg, in the late fifteenth century; in 1851 it was given the title of The Royal Lancaster Grammar School by Queen Victoria, as Duke of Lancaster. To this had been added in 1864 the Ripley Hospital, an orphanage foundation, later a secondary school for boys, a girls' grammar school established by the County Council in 1907 and the elementary schools, many of which were Church foundations. Three almshouses were named after their founders: Mayor John Gardyner (1485), Alderman William Penny (1720) and Mrs Ann Gillison (1790). Penny's Hospital was renovated and is still in use, but regrettably Gillison's Hospital was demolished in the late 1950s.

The city hospital was the Royal Lancaster Infirmary (established in 1896), while the Bay View Hospital (formerly the 'Union', or workhouse) included the 1909 Parkfield children's home. The cruelly-named Royal Albert Hospital for Idiots and Imbeciles and the County Asylum for the Insane completed the medical facilities.

Since the eighteenth century the castle had been a prison, initially for debtors, and also the site of public executions. A new Shire Hall now incorporated both civil and criminal courts, with the seventeenth century house nearby serving as the Judges' Lodging.

King's Own Royal Lancaster Regiment cap badge

The Cardwell reforms of the army had identified the Lancaster district of north Lancashire and Furness as the recruiting area for the 4th Regiment of Foot, which then became known as the King's Own (Royal Lancaster Regiment) or KORLR. Its regimental depot was Bowerham Barracks in the city (later St Martin's College of Education and now the Lancaster campus of the University of Cumbria). Like all other line regiments, it had two regular battalions, one serving at home and one abroad, a reserve (3rd) battalion, and two territorial battalions which were based at Ulverston (4th) and at Lancaster (5th). There was a unit of the Yeomanry based at White Cross, and the Royal Grammar School had a contingent of the Officers' Training Corps.

An armoured cruiser, HMS *Lancaster*, was affiliated to the city. Built by Armstrongs at Elswick, she displaced 9,800 tons, and was armed with fourteen 6-inch guns. She had an uneventful war. After a major refit at Chatham in 1914–15, she was sent to the Pacific as flagship, but after the destruction of Admiral Von Spee's squadron at the Falkland Islands, there was no further naval action there. A substantial number of Lancaster men served in other ships.

HMS Lancaster – naval-history.net

CHAPTER 2

The Coming of War

During the first half of 1914, the national press was mainly concerned with the approaching crisis in Ireland over home rule, economic problems and the increasing violence of the suffragette movement. As in other towns and cities the local press concerned itself with local matters, and the *Lancaster Guardian* was no exception. A weekly journal priced at a penny (1d), its front page was filled with advertisements (this was also true of *The Times*, which did not feature news on its front page until 1966), together with a column, headed 'Topical Talk', of the most lamentable jokes. Regular columns were entitled 'The Poultry Year' by Cockcrow, 'Dressmaking at home' by Sylvia, and 'Garden Gossip'; these were discontinued during the war.

Although there were only eight pages, almost a whole page was taken up by 'The Trey O'Hearts' – 'a novelised version of the motion picture drama', which was to be screened by the Picturedrome Cinema in Lower Church Street in early 1915. When this came to an end it was replaced by 'The Master Key', the synopsis of a western film.

The first piece of international news, in the issue of 6 June, was the collision in the St Lawrence River of the RMS *Empress of Ireland* with a Norwegian collier on 29 May 1914, with the loss of over 1,000 of her 1,400 passengers and crew. The resignation of the French government was news on 20 June, but the assassination, on 28 June, of the Archduke Franz Ferdinand and his wife in Sarajevo does not rate a mention, though a strike at Gillows' workshop does, as does the opening of the half-yearly Assizes.

Its rival weekly, the *Lancaster Observer*, not only reported the assassination, but published an informative article, setting the news in the context of recent Balkan history. Nevertheless its issue on 17 July was as inward-looking as ever. A large proportion of its eight pages was devoted to advertisements and to the entertainments available that week. A touring company was staging a play called 'The Shaughraun' at the Grand Theatre in St Leonardgate, while the programme at the Hippodrome in Dalton Square included a lady vocalist, a ventriloquist, a comedy boxing duo and an animated picture programme. This featured a 'prettily got-up story of the Willow Pattern'. The comedy acrobats Finland and Askey should have been on the bill, but had a motor cycle accident when travelling to Lancaster. The Picturedrome was showing a three-reel film entitled 'The Midnight Wedding', 'a fine drama dealing with court life in the kingdom of Savonia'. A free lecture at the Ashton Hall by the Honourable T.F. Rutherford of the New York City Bar offered a more demanding subject – 'Where are the Dead?', and there was an extensive review of a 'very readable' new book *Trout in Lakes and Reservoirs* by Ernest Phillips, formerly of Lancaster.

The grocers T.D. Smiths were advertising 'some particularly fine old English cheeses (made last Autumn) now in prime, ripe condition'. There were coach excursions by Red Rose Motors, while the London & North Western Railway ('the business and pleasure line') was offering travel to the Royal Lancashire Agricultural Show at Liverpool on the forthcoming Bank Holiday weekend. Over a hundred horses were sold at the July sales, fetching from 25 to 46 guineas each. Lancashire was to play Warwickshire in the County Cricket Championship at Lancaster's Lune Road ground, a match which attracted over 1,200 on the Friday, but which ended in a defeat for the home side by 173 runs. Warwickshire scored 346 and 142-4 declared, to which Lancashire could only reply with 128 and 187. There was a full club cricket programme for the Saturday, and the local football leagues were preparing for the September start to their new season. Life was normal.

On 24 July the *Observer* headline was AUSTRIA THREATENS SERVIA (this was then the usual spelling, soon to be discarded in favour of the more familiar Serbia). *'The murders of Archduke Franz Ferdinand and his wife have yet to be avenged, and Austrian public feeling has been artfully heated to make the punishment absolute and terribly deterrent in the future.'*

The demands made on Serbia by the Austro-Hungarian government were listed, with the observation that they could not be accepted, and that Serbia must fight. *'This would set the Balkans on fire again* [there had been two Balkan wars since 1912] *and in such a catastrophe Russia must take part.'* That such a conflict would disrupt trade was the only apparent concern for England.

A week later the headline (still only on page 4) was WAR BEGINS, without any clear suggestion that Britain might become involved. The *Observer* gave a detailed analysis of the situation in the Balkans, emphasising the racial disunity in the Austro-Hungarian Empire, and the possible intervention of Italy as well as Russia. *'This new war in fact is unique, and will be known to posterity as one of the most titanic and decisive the world has known.'* But it was a Balkan war, and the events of Monday's Bank Holiday loomed larger; these included the Lancaster regatta, and there were 'some holiday thoughts' under the heading BAG AND BAGGAGE.

In fact, Irish affairs featured in both newspapers with the reports of a local meeting of Unionists, addressed by Sir Edward Carson, who enjoined his supporters to have their arms at hand and to use them as necessary. Meanwhile the council was concerning itself with the matter of salary increases for its employees, and the sanitary committee with the control of an outbreak of scarlet fever.

The Police Court (as the magistrates' court was then known) had the usual list of petty offences: a man was fined ten shillings (10s) and costs for selling lottery tickets in the street, another two shillings and sixpence (2/6) for having a dog without a collar and another 5s for failing to produce his driving licence when required to do so. A motor cyclist was fined 20s and 9s costs (with the alternative of a month's hard labour) for driving to the danger of the public, and a man with a gun but no licence was fined 5s.

The *Guardian* headline on 8 August, COLONEL NORTH AND THE CRISIS, again referred to Ireland, but the *Observer* had the previous day announced: ENGLAND AT WAR. The violation of Belgian neutrality by Germany was the sole *casus belli*, and as a result:

'England has mobilised all her soldiers and sailors and the Territorials are embodied. The railways are under government control, recruiting is active, and a decided war fever animates

the United Kingdom. Lancaster is living in an atmosphere surcharged with the excitement of war, with dislocated businesses, irregular or missing trains, rising prices and other abnormalities.'

All male members of the St John's Ambulance Division offered their services at home or abroad, and several of its women members had made the same commitment.

Panic buying led to a rise in prices, for sugar in particular – the cost almost doubling from 1/6 to 2/6 per stone. Many grocers rationed their supplies, or sold only to regular customers; one shopkeeper recorded a grocery order which would have weighed two tons. The manufacturers James Williamson and Son and Messrs Storey Brothers, dependent on imported raw materials and on export orders, posted notices that they might have to close down their works, either partially or wholly. In the event, two of the cotton mills were closed in the next few weeks

The first news of the war referred to the 5th (Territorial) Battalion of the King's Own Royal Lancaster Regiment, which was due to begin

Soldiers of the 1st/5th Battalion, King's Own Royal Lancaster Regiment, on Railway guard duty, 1914.

its annual training with the West Lancashire Division of the Territorial Force near Kirkby Lonsdale on 2 August, the advance party having already set out. Orders received on a wet Sunday evening cancelled the training and recalled the units to base. Two days later, on 4 August, further orders were received, directing the 5th King's Own to Barrow-in-Furness, there to guard the docks and warships. The men were billeted in two large schools (readily available in the summer holidays) until they were relieved a week later and returned to Lancaster. Here they were billeted in the empty Carriage and Wagon Works on Caton Road until they were sent by train to Didcot, to guard the GWR line between Reading and Didcot. They moved on to Sevenoaks before, in February 1915, they embarked for France.

In August each newspaper began to carry a page on 'the great international crisis', to become 'the great European War', with details of military events, and a war diary: these of course lie outside the scope of this book. The political cartoons from *Punch* were reproduced at the head of the *Guardian* articles, highly critical of Germany, and of the Kaiser in particular. There were, however, three accounts written by Lancaster residents which described their difficulties in getting home from Germany, Austria and Belgium after war was declared.

CHAPTER 3

Casualties 1914–15

All those serving in the first two years of the war were volunteers and they suffered quite disproportionate losses. The 1st Battalion of the King's Own formed part of the initial British Expeditionary Force (BEF), and were soon in action at Mons and Le Cateau. Among the first to lose his life was their commanding officer, Lieutenant Colonel Alfred McNair Dykes, a veteran of the Boer War, along with three officers and eighty-three other ranks, who fell in the first weeks of the war. They included Private John Carney (1st King's Own) of Ridge Street.

Many of the early casualties were Lancaster men serving with other units. By the end of 1914 these included: Bombardier J. Wallbank of Earl Street (70 Battery, Royal Field Artillery), Lance Corporal R. Grayston of Gregson Road (12th Royal Lancers), Private E. Keen of Moorgate (Highland Light Infantry), Private Mangan of Charles Street (Manchester Regiment) and Private C. Adam of Back Queen Street (South Wales Borderers).

Lance Corporal R. Whymark of the 2nd King's Own was, like many of those initially posted as 'missing', later found to be a prisoner of war, but it was eventually discovered that he had died of wounds in a German hospital on 12 October. In December the Mayor proposed an 'adopt a PoW campaign' whereby parcels of food and clothing could be sent via the Red Cross. Eight months later he was able to report that forty-eight prisoners of the King's Own had been adopted by Lancaster families.

Lancaster men serving with the Royal Navy were also among the early casualties of war. They included three who died when their cruisers were torpedoed and sunk on 22 September 1914. The three 12,000 ton armoured cruisers *Aboukir, Hogue* and *Cressy* were on patrol in the North Sea when they were sighted by the German submarine *U9*. It torpedoed the *Aboukir*, which quickly capsized and sank. Her consorts stopped and lowered boats to rescue survivors, and were themselves sunk, with a total loss of over 1,400 lives. Of these, Gunner T.H. Adams of Sylvester Street had served aboard HMS *Aboukir* and Petty Officer C. Davies of Slyne Road and Torpedoman W. Wilson of Perth Street, aboard HMS *Cressy*. Later in the year Stoker J.E. Dunn of Charles Street was lost aboard HMS *Good Hope* at the Battle of Coronel, when she and HMS *Monmouth* (a sister ship of HMS *Lancaster*) were sunk by Admiral Graf Spee's more modern vessels SMS *Scharnhorst* and *Gneisenau*. Stoker R. Williams died in HMS *Hermes* when she was torpedoed in the Straits of Dover, while Stoker W. Peacock died in HMS *Lightning* and Chief Engine Room Artificer James Harker of Primrose Street, in Torpedo Boat 96, sunk off Gibraltar.

Private M.B. Taylor of Trafalgar Road (3rd Coldstream Guards) died of wounds on 8 September 1914 and Corporal R.H. Norris of Abbey Terrace, Scotforth was killed on 13 October 1914, when serving with the 1st Battalion of the King's Own. The son of a local policeman, Thomas Gardner of Rosebery Road, serving with the Scots Guards, was killed near Ypres in December 1914, aged 19, as was Trooper Hall of Prospect Street.

The 2nd Battalion King's Own returned from India, to see service briefly on the Western Front before being committed to the Gallipoli campaign in early 1915. There, casualties included Corporal L. Williams and Private R. Nicholson, both of Prospect Street and Private H. Park of Norfolk Street, all with the 2nd King's Own, as well as others of the new 6th Battalion. Another local casualty in this campaign was Private H. Fry of Derwent Road, serving with the 1st Manchester Regiment. Lieutenant T.S.I. Hall, grandson of Sir Thomas Storey, son of a former mayor, and an Old Lancastrian, had enlisted in the Royal Fusiliers in 1914. He was then commissioned into the King's Own, but was posted as missing, his death being presumed a year later.

In early 1915 the 5th Battalion of the King's Own went to France, and lost nine men in March and a further seven officers and 113 men in the Second Battle of Ypres in April and May. Their first death, however, had been that of Private James Hall of Pilling, a member of the Fleetwood platoon of the 5th King's Own. Having received his mobilisation papers on 4 August 1914, he shot himself with his service rifle the following day. The Coroner was highly critical of his action, declaring, 'The man had apparently taken his own life, and was perfectly sane. A soldier's duty is to serve his King and country, and it was an act of cowardice to take his own life.' He directed the jury to return a verdict of *felo de se* (suicide).

Another soldier died when hit by an express train when guarding a railway bridge near Reading before the battalion embarked for France.

Twelve men of 5th King's Own died soon after the battalion reached the front line in April 1915, and were buried together. They were Lance Corporal J. Harper of Wellington Street and Privates J. Nash (Albion Street), C. Whiteside (Park Square), J. Churchhouse (Marton Street), M. Farrell (Little John Street), T. Robinson (Aldcliffe Lane), W. Smith (Bridge Road), T. Clark (Lord Street), F. Eltoft (Derwent Road), F. Holding (Gage Street), R. Hothersall (Stanley Place) and R. Blackhurst (King's Arms Hotel, where his father was manager). Corporal B. Daly of Portland Street, serving with the 2nd Shropshire Light Infantry was also killed, as was Rifleman T. Clark of North Edward Street. Serving with the 1st King's Royal Rifles, he left a widow and four children.

Three men who died in May 1915 were 'all staunch friends', who had been employed at Gillows, and were all serving with the 5th King's Own. They were Privates H. Angus of Borrowdale Road, F.H. Lowe of Ullswater Road and J.P. Fairclough of Greenfield Street. In June the funeral of Private S. Milner of St Oswald Street (5th King's Own) at St John's Church was conducted by his brother, the Reverend John Milner. The 1st Battalion lost forty-three men killed and eighty wounded during May 1915, while others, posted as missing in action, were later found to be prisoners of war – more than 200 of them.

At the start of 1916 the *Guardian* published the photographs, with names and addresses, of over 200 local men who had died in 1915. They included (apart from those already mentioned): Captain Frank Miller Bingham (King's Own), of Lindow Square (a local doctor who is commemorated by a plaque in the Royal Lancaster Infirmary), Sergeant J. Gardner of Cheapside, and the first brothers to fall, Privates J. and G.F. Cuthbert of Cable Street. These had all served with the 5th

King's Own, but there were also men from the 2nd Battalion, as well as fourteen from the Seaforth Highlanders which had over 130 Lancaster men in its ranks. Two men of the Shropshire Light Infantry, Sergeant C. Dickinson of St Leonardgate, a former National School pupil, who left a widow and two young children, and Corporal B. Daly also were among those killed.

The war, and the casualties gave rise to a good deal of poetry published in both newspapers. The poet Laurence Binyon had been born in Lancaster in 1869, and early in the war composed his most famous lines 'For the Fallen', used since in remembrance services:

'They shall grow not old, as we that are left grow old. Age shall not weary them nor the years condemn. At the going down of the sun, and in the morning we will remember them.'

CHAPTER 4

The Home Front
1914–1916

By its very location in the north-west of England, Lancaster escaped some of the immediate impact of war. Units of the High Seas fleet had bombarded Scarborough, Whitby and Hartlepool, and the results of the shelling were screened in newsreels at the Hippodrome and Palladium cinemas. Zeppelin airships and Gotha bombers attacked targets in London and the south-east, causing civilian casualties. In early 1915 the German Submarine *U21* sank three freighters bound for Liverpool at the southern end of Morecambe Bay, though three more, heading for Glasgow, escaped. The *Observer* commented, *'The reality of war has been brought home to Lancaster people by an attack which caused alarm and some surprise, but nothing like terror. The fact that the west coast is vulnerable must now be recognised.'*

Lancaster quickly felt the more indirect effects of the war. The departure of men in large numbers to fight left large gaps in the labour force which had to be filled by men too old or unfit to fight, or by women. There is a widely held view that this war led to women's employment for the first time; this simply does not bear examination. For centuries women had worked on the land or in domestic service, then in nursing, and since the late eighteenth century in factories too. Women were traditionally employed in cotton spinning (weaving being regarded as men's work). What did change was in the types of work now done by women for the first time.

The first impact of the war was panic buying which led to food prices escalating. Flour rose from 1/9 to 2s per pound, and sugar doubled to 5d per pound. In response, advertisements for the grocer T.D. Smith identified their prices while reporting shortages; by 1915 the price of meat had risen, and many butchers were opening only three days each week.

Recruiting was a major issue and public meetings abounded. One was advertised in these words, *'Good Men from 25-30 years old are wanted for the 5th Battalion of the King's Own Royal Lancaster Regiment. Come to the Ashton Hall tomorrow.'* It was chaired by the Mayor, Councillor W. Briggs, and addressed by Colonel Lord Richard Cavendish, commanding officer of the 5th Battalion and Sir Norval Helme, MP for Lancaster, and was very successful in that 120 men came forward to add their names to the 360 who had already arrived at the regimental depot of Bowerham Barracks.

Ten squads were drilling there by the end of September and more men came forward in the succeeding weeks, so that over 3,000 had volunteered by the end of the year. These included fifty members of the staff of Gillows. The *Observer* commented:

Bowerham Barracks (LCM)

'There is a movement in Lancaster to form a Pals' Battalion. The idea is that groups of young fellows, companions in the region of sports, as club members or as fellow workmen should enlist together and continue the fellowship and companionship that has been so pleasant and helpful in civilian life.'

What was not foreseen was the distress when those who had enlisted to serve together also died together. Those who volunteered included *'professional men, salaried men, tradesmen, clerks, sportsmen and artisans – a company of which any town might be proud. The men who hang back are shirkers, and should be ashamed of themselves.'*

The mayor was Councillor William Briggs, who owned a pharmacy on Cheapside, although he was now retired. He had been a councillor since 1904, and took office as mayor in November 1913, a role which he was to fill for the next six years. He immediately launched an appeal

Councillor W. Briggs (LCM)

for a Relief Fund which was soon subsumed into the national Prince of Wales's Fund, which raised £3million in two months. Both newspapers carried lists of local subscriptions each week, headed by £25,000 from Lord Ashton, and a further £2,000 was raised in the first two weeks, with donations ranging from £50 down to five shillings. Collections at the parish church and at Scotforth St Paul on the first Sunday of the war totalled another £60.

The fund was intended to help those families who had lost their wages, and sometimes their homes, through a man's enlistment and some 300 Lancaster families had been assisted by the end of 1914. The unwieldy committee initially appointed (consisting of all 200 who had attended the inaugural meeting) soon delegated responsibility to sub-committees of ten, dealing with administration and finance. A ward sub-committee of five (with one woman member), and a women's committee of eight was chaired by the Mayoress, Mrs Briggs.

A similar fund for the relief of Belgian refugees was also set up, with Lord Ashton donating £5,000, and a further £5,000 raised by subscriptions. The first Belgian refugees arrived in Lancaster in October, and 'were given a cordial reception' at the Town Hall. They were then taken to a house in Dalton Square, which was to be a depot, and two houses in Dale Street were made available, the rents being paid by an anonymous donor. Mr and Mrs Pickard gave room at Oaklands for one couple. A few months later the town was to hear of the appalling treatment of a young Belgian boy of 14, who had lost his entire family in the German invasion. He had been taken prisoner, forced to dig trenches, and then had survived both a shooting and being bayonetted before escaping to England. In Lancaster he was adopted by the touring company of actors then appearing at the Grand Theatre.

In September 'there were reports prevalent in the district of Russian troops passing through the country from Scotland in trains with curtained doors and windows. While railway staffs had been on duty throughout the night because of the many troop trains, the Press Bureau discounted the story: 'the huge Russian army passing through the country at dead of night was a phantom, the figment of a community's disordered brain.'

At the first council meeting of the year, it was resolved to reinstate all employees who had volunteered for the forces, and that relief payments to dependents would be decided on the merits of each case.

The Mayoress inaugurated sewing parties of ladies who met at the Town Hall on three afternoons each week, to make garments for soldiers and for children in need. A sewing party at High Street Congregational Church made shirts, socks and other items of clothing which were sent to individual church members serving in the army, with a letter of thanks from Corporal J.J. Gilchrist of the King's Own being published.

The local Voluntary Aid Detachment met at the Old Town Hall (now the City Museum) to arrange for the setting-up and staffing of a hospital in Lancaster (eventually established at Bowerham). Mr and Mrs Gillow offered Leighton Hall as a hospital, and Mr and Mrs Pickard offered Oaklands as a convalescent home. Bowerham School was taken over to be used as a hospital, the pupils being transferred (with some overcrowding) to the former Sulyard Street School, recently closed when the new school at Dallas Road opened.

Subscriptions provided a motor ambulance with the name 'Luck to Loyne' (the town motto) with a second vehicle being provided by Lady Ashton. The war did bring some benefit to local industry, with early orders including one for 400 pairs of boots for the French army from J. Cockerill and Son of Great John Street. The firm continued to make boots for the British Army throughout the war. Another order was for 300 field kitchens for the BEF from Lune Valley Engineering.

The army did not only need men, it required horses, both as remounts for the cavalry and as draught animals. The former Artillery Drill Hall in Dallas Road had stabling for 1,400 beasts, with 'shoeing carried out early and late'. Any 'respectable person' might have the use of one of the horses, in return for its keep, to maintain its fitness in 'a good, hard condition'. The horses were sent in batches to Dover or Southampton to be shipped to France. Fifty years later, the building (since demolished) became the British Road Services depot.

In November 1914, the council unanimously decided to re-elect Councillor Briggs as Mayor.

'With a high sense of duty he assented to the request of his colleagues that he should continue in office to carry out the work begun on the outbreak of war. It would have been difficult for any other member of the council to take up the threads of the multitudinous affairs which Mr Briggs has in hand. His Worship has indicated that this should be a "business year", and asks that he be spared the duty of attending outside meetings and functions.'

Throughout the next five years he displayed amazing energy and devotion to his duties. At this point also the council presented to Mr and Mrs Briggs an engraved silver salver to mark their 25th wedding anniversary, while he gave to the town a chain for the Mayoress.

'From a gold chain, whose links are Lancashire red roses, hangs a pendant with the arms of the borough, surrounded by opals, sapphires and rubies.'

Mrs W. Briggs (LCM)

The provision of 'comforts for the soldiers' became a local industry. At Scotforth St Paul's Church a group of fifty women knitted socks and balaclava helmets. The first consignment went to the 1st King's Own, already in France, and another consignment, which consisted of cigarettes, tobacco, socks, notebooks and pencils was sent by the Mayor; a similar batch went to HMS *Lancaster*. Others went to the troops at the internment camp and its inmates, and to the 3rd and the 5th King's Own with footballs, boxing gloves, and playing cards featuring in them. A later innovation was the collection and dispatch of eggs for wounded soldiers from February 1915. Forty-five were collected the first week, and two or three hundred each succeeding week. This enterprise continued to be reported weekly throughout the war, with a record total of 1,546 in May 1915.

While there was an increasing shortage of labour in factories and on farms, local firms were soon advertising 'business as usual', led by the dress shop Chirnsides (which only closed in 2012), but soon copied by others. Advertisements made increasing use of references to the war to sell their goods, often with suggestions for gifts to be sent by relatives to their soldiers. These became more frequent as Christmas approached. 'What to give your soldier son?' asked Leightons, offering a service watch as the answer. Manserghs had laid in a large stock of coloured army blankets, priced at 3/9, 5/9 and 6/3, offering these as 'an ideal gift'. Simpsons of Brock Street suggested winter underwear for soldiers and sailors, while the opticians Hines stocked a trench periscope 'approved by the War Office' and costing 7/6. Leightons were later to make the same offer, 'to save lives in the trenches'. Dri-Ped leather soles were 'for active service at the front – even the mud of Flanders cannot penetrate them' or, more simply, as 'Tommy's sole comfort'.

Other more prosaic suggestions were for Lifebuoy soap ('Send him a tablet today') or Beecham's pills, but the most persistent were those for Zam-Buk, 'a unique herbal remedy'. 'What the war teaches us is the vital need for Zam-Buk', it was claimed. It purported to be a remarkable panacea, apparently efficacious against 'bruises, burns, scalds, poisonous wounds, ulcers, rashes, piles' and other ailments. It called upon Private Abraham Acton VC of 1st Borders to vouch for its worth, quoting him as saying, 'I always have a pack in my knapsack'.

In February 1915, the jewellers James Rhodes of Penny Street were

Zam-Buk

advertising brooches of the lion crest (the collar badge of the King's Own), at a shilling in white metal or 12/9 in gold, with the exhortation 'everyone should wear one and give one to a friend'.

Once the former Carriage and Wagon Works in Caton Road had been evacuated by the troops in late 1914, it became a camp for German internees. There was a capacity for 1,700 and of the initial 800, most were Germans or Austrians working in the country (especially as waiters in hotels) or the crews of German ships in British ports at the

German PoWs.

outbreak of war. The first batch, of 140, arrived from Liverpool, guarded during the journey by men of the Cheshire Regiment, though the camp was staffed by the 3rd (Reserve battalion) Welsh Fusiliers. Of a new batch of forty prisoners, seven were waiters from hotels in Carlisle. They had a food allocation of bread or biscuit, meat, vegetables, sugar, butter or margarine and tea or coffee – which some thought over-generous, especially by comparison with that available to the wives and children of soldiers at the front. The Commandant was Colonel Cholmondley, and one of his officers was Lieutenant Robert Graves, author of *The Greek Myths, I, Claudius* and *Claudius the God*, who recounts his memories in his autobiography *Goodbye to All That*.

The camp was, in the early weeks of the war, a source of great interest to the editor of the *Guardian*, who wrote in September:

'From the field above the Wagon Works, the prisoners may be seen taking exercise. They seem to be in high spirits, probably because they are far from the seat of war, and enjoy themselves playing various games, football being one of these. Some are keen on dancing, and there is a German band to supply the music. Those who can afford to do so patronise a dry canteen.'

A week later, he wrote:

'Lancaster, as a camp for German and Austrian prisoners, is attaining a notoriety never anticipated. The arrival on Saturday of a batch of manacled aliens from Manchester, escorted by a detachment of stalwart policemen armed with rifles, created quite a stir.'

And another week he wrote:

'There have been further drafts of prisoners to the Wagon Works compound this week, from as far south as Hanley, and as far north as Newcastle and Carlisle. Arrangements are being made for religious services to be held on Sundays for various groups, according to their beliefs. Last Sunday a sacred concert was given by a number of Lancaster vocalists.'

When Colonel Cholmondley was transferred to a similar appointment in Shrewsbury, he was replaced by Colonel Ansley of the Loyal North Lancashire Regiment, and a guard of National Reservists took over from the Welsh Fusiliers, posted to France. Under the new regime some of the prisoners began squabbling among themselves, and four were ordered to serve three days solitary confinement in the police cells, situated in the basement of the Town Hall. A new system was introduced, whereby picked men were appointed as captains, responsible for the good behaviour of their charges.

A temporary theatre was set up in one of the huts, where 'entertainments are given by prisoner-artistes, who include several talented acrobatic troupes, jugglers and comedians'. Comforts, both for the detainees and for the troops guarding them were provided. The Vicar of Lancaster was one of those who conducted services, while at

Christmas 1914 a service was held by a Lutheran pastor, one of the detainees. There were carols sung by their choir, selections from Handel's 'Messiah', played by their band, and a traditional Christmas meal of turkey and plum pudding.

A letter from Private F. Carter of Dorrington Road referred to the unofficial Christmas Truce of 1914, when, *'The German Huns came over to our trenches (the lines were only eighty yards apart) and wished us a Merry Christmas, and sang God Save the King. We exchanged curios, and gave them fags.'*

The year 1915 opened with the traditional New Year's party for 800 old people given by Mr H.L. Storey in the Drill Hall, a tea followed by entertainment. A similar event was provided by the nurses of 24 (West Lancashire) Voluntary Aid Detachment, held in the hospital at Bowerham barracks for the wounded soldiers there.

At the spring Assizes, there were only three cases to be heard: a postman accused of stealing three postal orders of a total value 10/6 was given three months imprisonment with hard labour, while a second charge of theft was dismissed. A retired solicitor of Blackpool was convicted of the murder of his clerk, but was found to be insane, and was consigned to be kept in custody as a criminal lunatic.

Both local newspapers maintained details of the progress of the war, and both were very gung-ho about the subject, despite the huge casualty lists. GERMAN ARMIES ROUTED was a headline in August. The local tailors, Redmaynes, started a competition in early 1915 to guess the date on which the war would end, offering 200 two guinea suits as prizes. A few weeks later it was revealed that most forecast the autumn of 1915, though one pessimist identified 10 December 1934. No winner was identified when the Armistice was eventually signed.

DORA, the Defence of the Realm Act, provided not only for the military control of the railways and the registration of aliens, but for restrictions on civilian life, some unexpected. There were instructions on action in the event of an air raid, the alarm being given by ten blasts on the fire siren. People were advised to stay indoors and to take shelter in basements. Owners of carrier or homing pigeons had to register with the police, while opening hours and sales in public houses were reduced and there were limitations on street lighting and on railway services. Anyone in possession of arms, ammunition or explosives had to report this to the police.

There was a spy scare in April 1915 when a man named Henry Bates was seen sketching Carlisle Bridge. Arrested by the sentries, he was taken to the police station 'with a large crowd following'. The next day he was taken to Bowerham Barracks, where the commanding officer, Colonel Duffin, examined the case and ordered his release.

In the early months of the war there was a good deal of consideration of what activities and events might be deemed 'inappropriate'. The first was cancellation of the Lancaster Agricultural Show in the first week in September. Later the mayoral dinner in November to mark the re-election of Councillor Briggs was abandoned, and a modest luncheon was substituted. The Vale of Lune Rugby Club cancelled its fixtures and Lancaster Town FC followed suit in April, despite having won promotion in the season just ended. Cricket remained unaffected and the William Smith Festival for children took place at Easter 1915, and in the following years, on Giant Axe, as usual.

Recruiting had been good in 1914, with about 3,000 men joining the colours, but fell off in 1915. Several attempts were made to boost the numbers, with specific pleas for recruits for the 3rd and the new 11th battalions of the King's Own. At the same time, War Office posters were stressing the need for motor drivers, blacksmiths, butchers and bakers. An official poster published in early 1915 asked:

FOUR QUESTIONS TO EMPLOYERS

As an employer, have you seen that every fit man under your control has been given every opportunity of enlisting?
1. Have you encouraged your men to enlist by offering to keep their positions open?
2. Have you offered to help them in any other way if they will serve their country?
3. Have you any men still in your employ who ought to enlist? Our present prosperity is largely due to men already in the field, but to maintain it and to end the war, we must have more men. Your country will appreciate the help you give.
MORE MEN ARE WANTED TODAY
4. What can YOU do?
GOD SAVE THE KING

The impact on local industries of the loss of so many employees reached serious levels: by early 1915 over 600 of Williamson's workforce and 300 of Storeys had volunteered for military service, while Gillows had also suffered severely, and it was suggested that these firms should now be exempt from recruiting drives. The *Observer* commented:

> *'Lancaster has done so well in the way of recruiting that a new danger faces the town, namely the possibility of the principal works being closed as a result of so many men having joined His Majesty's forces. The staple industry of Lancaster is so highly specialised, and the work so carefully organised that if certain workpeople are absent, others must be idle. There comes a point in such industries when the removal of men jeopardises the continuance of the industry altogether. This point has been reached in Lancaster, and it is well that the fact should be faced. The closing down of the works would be disastrous for Lancaster, and prolonged distress would be certain.'*

The Mayor took up the issue, sending first a telegram to the War Office, which responded that enlistment was entirely a matter for the men themselves, and that no involvement of the War Office could be contemplated. The matter reached Lord Kitchener, Minister for War, who responded angrily, indicating that recruiting was the first and indeed the only priority. Councillor Briggs then wrote at length to the Prime Minister, without success. Later an amendment to the Factories and Workshops Act exempted any works where 'the Secretary of State is satisfied that, by reason of the loss of men through enlistment, exemption is necessary to secure the carrying-on of work which is required in the national interest'. It is not clear whether Lancaster's products could be so defined, but two cotton mills had already closed. Soon the Postmaster announced that 'because of a serious depletion of staff due to the war', he would have to close an hour early – at 8pm instead of 9pm! He later announced a reduction in the Sunday opening hours.

The Cadet battalion of the King's Own, which had been proposed in the early weeks of the war, was given War Office approval in May 1915. According to the Press:

'A comprehensive programme has been arranged, and the movement has every prospect of success and will eventually take its place as one of the town's institutions. The youth of the town have now an excellent opportunity to show their patriotism by undergoing a system of drill and physical training that will benefit themselves and prepare them for eventualities.'

The Mayor (who else?) accepted the position of honorary colonel, and the chairmanship of a committee to support the movement and guarantee its finances. Provision was made for four companies of from thirty to a hundred cadets each, open to 'respectable youths' of 14–17 years of age for whom uniform and equipment would be provided. They would drill every Tuesday and Friday evenings, from 7.45, at Giant Axe Field if the weather was fine, and in the Drill Hall in Phoenix Street if wet. They provided a guard of honour for the recruiting meetings, and a photograph shows thirty cadets at a church parade at the parish church.

At a council meeting in May 1915, Councillor Jemmison protested indignantly that relatives wishing to say goodbye to their sons leaving by train for France had been denied access to the Castle Station by railway staff. He proposed a resolution be sent to the stationmaster in protest, and had the support of a number of colleagues. Instead it was agreed that the Mayor should see if a system of passes could be arranged. He later reported that he had had two meetings with the district superintendent who had said that he would do everything in his power to enable relatives to be allowed on the platform. There was the matter of danger in overcrowded platforms, and the station was in the control of the military when troops were boarding the trains.

The sinking of the Cunard liner RMS *Lusitania* by a German submarine off the south coast of Ireland on 7 May 1915 involved several Lancastrians, who later recounted their ordeal. Mrs Harriet Plank had lived in Skerton for twenty-one years before she, her husband and their two daughters left for Canada in 1913. She had decided to visit her mother, taking with her the younger daughter, aged seven. When the torpedoes struck the ship, they went up on deck, where the mother threw her daughter down into a lifeboat, some seven feet below, and jumped in herself. They were transferred first to a fishing smack and then to a steam trawler which took them into Queenstown.

She had heartrending stories to tell of the tragedies they had witnessed in the lifeboat, including a man dying with his head in her lap, a distraught mother crying for her lost baby, and a little girl who had lost both parents. Steward William Rose (son of the steward of Lancaster's County Club) was serving lunch to the second class passengers when the ship was hit. He and his colleagues helped to get the passengers into the boats until told to save themselves. *'The discipline was admirable,'* he told the *Observer. 'There was no panic, no disorder.'* He was so long in the water that he was unconscious when picked up.

Bell-boy Benjamin Holton, aged 14, had only left the Ripley Hospital the previous year. He told how he had dived over the port side and got onto a floating dog-kennel which supported him until he was picked up by the armed trawler *Indian Empire.* As 195 Americans were among those lost, there was an acrimonious exchange of diplomatic messages between President Woodrow Wilson and the German Foreign Minister which, while it did not immediately lead to the entry of the USA into the war, certainly made that more likely.

There was, later in the year, a similar experience for a Mrs Wrathall. She, with her husband and two daughters had also left for Canada before the war, and she too, with their younger daughter, aged nine, had been visiting her mother in Lancaster. Their return passage was aboard the Allan line ship *Hesperian* which, with 300 passengers and 200 crew, was bound from Liverpool to Montreal. A German submarine torpedoed the vessel off the south coast of Ireland as Mrs Wrathall and her daughter were preparing for bed. Half-dressed, they rushed up on deck and were put into a lifeboat which took them to Queenstown. Wounded Canadian soldiers who were returning home assisted in the evacuation, but as the ship did not sink immediately, the captain and some crew members remained on board. A tug took the vessel in tow, making for Queenstown, but the following day she sank before reaching port. Thirteen crew members and twelve passengers were lost.

When the Moss Line steamer *Minieh* was sunk in 1916, Chief Officer J.B. Morris of Rossmoyne Road was among those saved.

Also in May the Lancaster Agricultural Society decided to cancel its forthcoming Show, 'as the only wise course to adopt – perhaps the only possible one. Farmers are not in the mood for preparing stock for shows, and in many instances have not the time or the labour for such purposes. Agricultural shows are valuable institutions in normal circumstance, but in this period of world conflict they would be out of place.' The death of their secretary, Lieutenant Robert Gardner, no doubt rendered the decision easier.

By mid-1915 there were growing demands for conscription, a contentious issue, and while it had not been introduced by the end of the year, a national registration scheme seemed to bring it closer. In August 152 enumerators began the task of visiting some 30,000 individuals in the area to register them 'tactfully, and in a spirit of helpfulness'. The King's Own, it was claimed, needed at least thirty men per week, while the number coming forward each week was only five. It was alleged that there were some 1,000 fit and single young men in the area, branded as 'shirkers and slackers, earning fat wages'.

That this was a widespread phenomenon was indicated by a meeting of all Lancashire mayors in June, called by the Lord Lieutenant, Lord Shuttleworth, to encourage the formation of Volunteer Training Corps detachments, to provide basic training and to take over some roles, such as guard duty, from the military. Another proposal was for civilian recruiting committees to assist the military authorities in their work. Councillor Briggs put this to a public meeting in Lancaster, which resolved to set up such a committee. A reduction in the height requirement led to the formation of an 11th Battalion of the King's Own, known as 'the Bantams', while the War Office was advertising for MT drivers for the Army Service Corps. The Royal Army Medical Corps decided to set up a County Palatine Division, and Mr G.L. Shaw, a teacher at Bowerham school, was an early volunteer. Seven local policemen volunteered to join the military police.

There was also evidence of some feeling of doubt about the war – the Centenary Brotherhood asked 'is the war worthwhile?' and the local Band of Hope and Temperance Union condemned the rising consumption of alcohol, looking forward to people asking 'Why do we have public houses at all?' A later meeting resolved to petition the government to prohibit the manufacture, import, export and sale of all alcohol, foreshadowing Prohibition in the United States.

The newspapers also reported a steep increase in child crime, with twenty-five cases in 1915 compared with only three the previous year.

This was attributed to the absence of the fathers. There were also increasing numbers of cases of drunkenness by women.

As recruiting lagged, the local newspapers gave prominence to local families who had numerous members in uniform. Among these were the Bradleys of Cable Street with five sons (all former employees of Williamson's Lune Mills) serving with the 5th King's Own. The Corless family of Beresford Street had a father (William, with the 3rd King's Own), and five sons in uniform. These were Corporal William (10th Royal Field Artillery) and Privates John (1st King's Own), Robert, Albert, and Richard (5th King's Own).

Mr B. Hall of Skerton also had five sons in uniform while the Butterworth family of Green Street, Bulk, had five sons serving, four of whom were to meet their deaths in action. They were William, a private with the York and Lancaster Regiment (October 1914); Charles, a lance sergeant with the 2nd King's Own (May 1915); Hugh, a private with the 2nd King's Own (Aug 1915) and John, a private with the 5th King's Own (June 1917). All had been pupils of the National School.

A happier note was to be seen in the council resolution congratulating Professor A.C. Seward MA FRS on his election as Master of Downing College, Cambridge. A member of a Lancaster family with an ironmonger's business, he was educated at the Royal Grammar School before going on to St John's College Cambridge, and then held Fellowships at St John's and Emmanuel Colleges. He was then appointed Professor of Botany at the University.

The question of women's employment was again raised, and was equally controversial. Claims that men could be released from employment if replaced by older men or even by women were rejected by those who felt that women could not do the work, or at the very least would require training. One shopkeeper wrote to say that he had lost thirty per cent of his staff and that 'the work cannot be done by women'. The secretarial school De Bears, claimed in January 1915 that 'the demand for qualified girls is now greater than ever', but this is not borne out by the situations vacant column. It is very likely, however, that firms requiring girl secretaries would have approached the organisation direct. The advertisements for women staff were almost always for domestic servants, or for workers in millinery or dressmaking. Albion Mills, advertising for workpeople, did specify girls in their early teens (recent school-leavers), but the spinning mills had been a traditional workplace for girls for a century and more.

Again the *Observer* had an editorial on the subject, headed WOMEN AND THE WAR:

> *'Men being at the war, we have to rely on women doing work ordinarily done by men. For a generation, women have steadily avoided agricultural employment, in spite of ever-increasing wages and lighter duties, until now the pert village girl scorns the milk pail, the piggeries and farmhouse labour.'*

A meeting of the Lancashire Farmers' Association in April, however, showed the continuing resistance to the employment of women, other than from the farming families, claiming that there were few who were suited to the work. One farmer claimed that a woman assigned to his farm left 'because she had a poodle dog and there was no bath for it'. The chairman said that farmers should not be too hard on women, who came with the very best intentions, but conceded that the average farmer was hard to convince. At a general meeting in May, again on the theme of agriculture, it was resolved that farmers should ask themselves 'In what way could I possibly make use of women on my farm?'

By 1916, however, sheer need was beginning to overcome prejudice. Women had never worked in the White Cross Mill of Storeys (though they had been employed in the spinning mills on Moor Lane), but they now were to be seen in the warehouses and in office work.

A new diversion here was the manufacture of shells, again with a largely female workforce. At Williamson's too, the loss of so many male employees meant that women had to join the workforce. Gillows were also beginning to diversify to meet the demands of the war, with the manufacture of ammunition boxes, crates and aircraft wings, and here too women were employed.

As Christmas 1915 approached, there was renewed activity in providing comforts: the mayoress's fund provided turkeys (and 100 pairs of socks) for men of the 5th King's Own and 10 Battery Royal Field Artillery at the front, while the Post Office was said to be 'snowed under' with parcels sent by relatives. There were requests for footballs, mouth organs and books from officers commanding the troops.

Women Workers at Storeys (LCM)

Shell making at Storeys (LCM)

A request for owners of motor vehicles to donate these for use by the military brought immediate responses from Dr J. Aitken of the Dalton Square practice, and from shop owner Mr A.H. Mansergh. An ambulance fund was established, with Lord Ashton again heading the list of subscribers with £5,000.

The castle closed as a civil prison in 1915, with the German internees being moved there from the Carriage and Wagon Works. A letter from the Ministry of Munitions to the council had proposed the siting of a factory in Lancaster, and in August the council was told that 'Lancaster will become a munitions centre'. The Caton Road site was opened as a National Projectile Factory in 1916, turning shells rough-made in Barrow-in-Furness and sending them on to the new National Filling Factory at White Lund.

Here they were filled with TNT – a much more dangerous process. For security reasons, the opening of the factory was not reported in the press, though there were weekly reports of the Munitions Court, where workers were charged with offences. They were working under government regulations, stricter than in other industries (while being paid significantly higher wages) and could be fined for being insufficiently industrious, or insubordinate, for sleeping at work (usually on the night shift) for refusal to work, or for absenteeism. The *Observer* commented critically of the sympathy of other workers for those fined, and the practice of collections to help pay fines.

> *'This is a false attitude for anyone to take. Rather should the spirit be fostered among the workpeople that those who would not observe the regulations drawn up for the general safety are traitors to their fellows, and should be ostracised, and brought to a right frame of mind.'*

Even more serious was the possession of cigarettes, tobacco or matches which could, and did, incur prison sentences of up to six months. Some 8,000 workers were employed in the two plants, three-quarters of them women. For them special conditions were imposed so that they could work with the utmost degree of safety. Fireproof overalls, caps, veils, gloves and respirators were provided. A canteen provided free hot meals day and night, and there was a women's rest room, staffed by women doctors and nurses to treat minor injuries and to provide

National Projectile Factory canteen. (LCM)

periodic medical examinations. Hot baths and free milk were also made available. A hostel for the women workers was opened by the Girls' Friendly Society.

One of them, a young woman crane operator, was killed in a fall at the Caton Road factory in July 1916, and a male colleague met with a similar accident in the following year. The Coroner recorded a verdict of accidental death in each case.

The recruiting campaigns of mid-1915 were intense, with daily outdoor meetings in Market Square during a two-week period, backed by a cinema van showing pictures of a devastated Belgium and 'the wicked work of the Huns'. Further meetings with the Co-operative workers and at the Grand Theatre were held, but in all only thirty new recruits came forward. It was said that *'if all the local farmers, small employers and shopkeepers had sent to the colours as good a percentage of men as the two great works in this town, we should not need a recruiting campaign in Lancaster. But 3,500 men of military age still remain at home, and of these a thousand could join the army immediately.'*

In September 1915, the *Observer*, under a headline of UNIVERSAL SERVICE made these comments:

'Unless we muster all the men capable of finishing the war triumphantly, the tremendous sacrifices made, and to be made, may be virtually useless. Lord Kitchener's last call was for 300,000 more men. The cry from the trenches is for more and more. We must assume that they will not be forthcoming. These million absentees from the warfields are the spoiled children of our pampered age. They are young, able-bodied, eager for all the good things going. They are thriving on high wage; yet blatant demanders of higher wages and of less work for those wages. Never have men enjoyed such good times as these are enjoying, while their old mates – many of them married – are giving life, limb and liberty for their country, and for these recreants. This astonishing anomaly is caused by our voluntary system.'

A strange editorial in the *Observer*, on 5 November, was based on a profoundly pessimistic view of the post-war world, which assumed a death toll of British men of fifteen million. The editor wrote:

'After the war aged men, weaklings and children will alone represent the male race. Women will have all the world's work to do. They will have to toil incessantly, to keep the State going, and to earn the gigantic sums needed to pay interest and redemption of the loans, also to find capital for new enterprises. That means woman will no longer pursue woman's natural career as wife and mother. She will be a machine, ever grinding out the iron necessities of corporate life. The truly feminine will disappear. They are born for love and home. Lacking husbands and offspring, life will have no meaning for them. In the utter change of society they will become lost creatures – for society exists because of sex. Already the shadows of a lost civilisation grow around us. The world before August 4th 1914 has disappeared, and a new monster age arrives.'

In the event, the British death toll fell a little short of three-quarters of a million – hideous enough, and causing major problems, but a long way short of this projected cataclysm.

The next week saw the re-election of the Mayor, for a third term. The council was unanimous in asking Councillor Briggs to remain in office, assuming that 'the year upon which the Mayor has entered will not be less arduous than the two just passed. There is every likelihood that before twelve months hence the war will have reached the end, and it is fitting that Mr Briggs should be at the head of affairs when the town celebrates the declaration of peace. No one deserves honour, support and sympathy more than Mr Briggs. Except it be Mrs Briggs who, as Mayoress, has discharged the duties of the office with ability and charm. She has not spared herself in devoted labour for the soldiers, sailors and men in training for active service. It is her desire that one thousand pairs of socks for local soldiers should be provided by Christmas. Local women should see that the request is cheerfully complied with.'

Her fund enabled comforts to be sent to all serving with 5th King's Own and the Lancaster Battery of the Royal Field Artillery at Christmas, including a turkey dinner. The pupils of Dallas Road School and the Boys' National School also sent parcels to their former pupils.

The council then turned to matters of administration. Contracts for the extension of the gasworks were accepted, as was a proposal for the purchase of motor buses to work alongside the trams, which were proving unprofitable. A deficit on the year of over £1,400 was declared at the meeting of the shareholders of the Lancaster & District Tramways Company. An extension to the waterworks was also considered, and then the membership of the various council committees was decided.

Later in the month the council took the decision to rename Germany Street (which ran from Parliament Street to St Leonardgate and Caton Road) as 'inappropriate'. While this met with general approval, the new name, of Bulk Road did not. The shooting by the Germans of nurse Edith Cavell earlier in the year ('so foully done to death') had been met with massive disapproval nationwide, and it was thought that Cavell Avenue might have been chosen.

Later in the month a concert was held in the Ashton Hall by Mr Aldous's choir (he was music master at the two grammar schools) to raise money for the Mayoress's fund to provide comforts for local soldiers. The sum raised was £18 9s. Lieutenant T.W. Forshaw VC who, when working as a teacher in Lancaster, had been a member of the choir appeared, in uniform, to sing two baritone solos. This was the signal for 'a great burst of applause from audience and choir alike'.

The Town Clerk then read the text of an official address of congratulation on the award of his decoration. The address, illuminated with the arms of the borough, and with the Lancaster red rose was then presented by the Mayor to Lieutenant Forshaw.

The year ended with a remarkable statement to the Council by local architect and town planner, Mr T.H. Mawson. He was to give a lecture the following month on Athens, Rome and Edinburgh, but now asserted that 'Lancaster was potentially superior' to these three cities. It is hardly surprising that this was greeted with some scepticism!

CHAPTER 5

Lancaster Schools

In 1914, Lancaster had more than a dozen elementary schools, of which over half were Church of England Schools owing their existence to the National Society (St Mary's, St John's, St Anne's, St Thomas's, Christ Church, St Paul's, St Luke's and the National Schools for boys and girls), two Roman Catholic schools (St Peter's and St Joseph's), and the council schools of Bowerham, Greaves, the Quay and Skerton. A new council school on Dallas Road replaced the former Sulyard Street school. Most of these still exist today as the city's primary schools. There were also the orphanage and school of the Ripley Hospital foundation, the independent Friends' School on Castle Hill and the two grammar schools, for boys and girls. The historic Lancaster Royal Grammar School was endowed in 1472 'to educate boys in grammar, freely', an ethos which remains today. The Girls' Grammar School was a recent foundation (1907) and was housed at first in the Storey Institute, its new, purpose-built premises in Regent Street being opened just after the start of the war, in September 1914, with, understandably, very little ceremony.

During the early months of the war, the headmasters of the Lancaster elementary schools submitted to the newspapers lists of their former pupils who had volunteered. The largest of the schools was the Boys' National School; over a thousand former pupils served in the war. By February 1917 six members of the teaching staff had been commissioned: they were second lieutenants W. Brash, S. Armstrong, R. Irving, W. Pinch, F.H. Smith and W.H. Metcalfe, of whom the first three had already been killed in action. The names of 155 who gave

Ripley Hospital (LCM)

their lives are recorded on a memorial, now in the chapel of Ripley St Thomas Academy. The National School was merged with Ripley after the Second World War, when it was felt that an orphanage foundation was no longer required, and Ripley became simply a school.

The Ripley memorial lists thirty-three names of former pupils who fell (the number who served is not recorded, but Ripley was, apart from the Friends' School, the smallest of the schools with only 150 boys on the roll). Records show that the majority of these came from Liverpool, where the Ripley family was based, but the brothers Higginson, from Spring Garden Street joined the 5th King's Own. Both lost their lives, Henry in 1916, while Samuel, missing since May 1915, was eventually presumed dead. His name is listed on the Menin Gate at Ypres, along with others with no known grave.

Among others who fell, one was with the Canadian Contingent, having emigrated in 1913, while others served with the Royal Engineers, the Royal Warwickshire Regiment, the Royal Horse Guards, the Royal Field Artillery and the Machine Gun Corps. One of the last to lose his life was Able Seaman J.H. Railton of Skerton, lost when the sloop HMS *Anchusa* was torpedoed in July 1918 when on convoy escort duty. Two were awarded the Military Medal and one the Military Cross.

Awards to former Bowerham pupils include one Victoria Cross, three Military Crosses, four Distinguished Conduct Medals and seven Military Medals. The Bowerham memorial (still in place in the school's library) lists all of these among the 578 serving with the colours, of whom eighty-eight did not survive. The list includes a number of names in blue, indicating females, but whether these were serving with the Voluntary Aid Detachment or First Aid Nursing Yeomanry or with the new women's services, perhaps as drivers, cannot be ascertained.

A plaque in memory of Second Lieutenant R. Irving, a former pupil of the Royal Grammar School, later a teacher at Greaves School was moved to Lancaster Castle School (now Central Lancaster High School) when it replaced Greaves. He enlisted with 5th King's Own on the outbreak of war, had been wounded at Ypres in 1915 and reached the rank of sergeant in 1916 when he was commissioned. He died in the Somme offensive, on 2 August 1916.

At St Thomas's School, a roll of honour was unveiled by the Mayor on Empire Day in May 1916; it displayed 332 names flanked by figures representing Truth and Justice. Eventually over 700 former pupils of this school served, of whom ninety-five did not return. In September 1918, the presentation of the Military Medal was made on the steps of the Town Hall by the Mayor to Bombardier R. Jackson aged 21, of nearby Brock Street, with the headmaster and pupils of St Thomas's in attendance. He was one of seven former pupils to win this award, with one Military Cross and two Distinguished Conduct Medals. (The school later became a secondary school for girls after the 1944 reorganisation, subsequently joining the Ripley school to form a co-educational Church of England high school.)

A similar memorial was unveiled at Christ Church School by the Vicar, the Reverend Ker-Cooper. Here there were figures of Fame and Saint George either side of a list of 352 former pupils and ten members of staff, thirty of whom had already given their lives by early 1917.

The most complete list of former pupils is that of the Royal Grammar School. No fewer than 141 former pupils were in the armed forces in December 1914. It can be deduced from the ranks they then held that at least forty-eight were either regular or reserve soldiers –

School House, Lancaster Royal Grammar School. (LRGS)

six were majors and thirteen were captains, with several sergeants and corporals.

Of these the most senior were Major O.C. Borrett of the King's Own, who by 1918 held the rank of brigadier general, with the CMG, DSO and bar and the Croix de Guerre (he eventually reached the rank of lieutenant general and was colonel of the regiment from 1926-44) and Lieutenant Commander J.B. Pulliblank RN. He won the DSO and later rose to the rank of rear admiral. As an engineer he had done well to overcome the prejudice in favour of seaman branch officers.

Among the captains was W.R.W. Deed, a master at the school, who joined the 5th Battalion of the King's Own in 1912, and who, in 1914, had become the first contingent commander of the school's Officers' Training Corps. On the outbreak of war he joined the battalion, handing over command of the corps to Captain S.A. Pakeman. Captain Deed served on the Western Front (sending frequent letters back to the school) until 1917, when he took up a training role. Captain Pakeman was later to serve with the Gloucestershire Regiment, winning the Military Cross in 1917.

Another master was Lieutenant B.H. Binks, a former housemaster and teacher of Modern Languages (he had achieved a first class degree at Queens' College, Cambridge) who joined the 11th King's Own and was killed in France in October 1916.

Among the new volunteers, most had left the school six or eight years earlier. They were likely to be established in a career, very possibly married and perhaps with young children. These were the very men who saw it as their patriotic duty to respond to Kitchener's appeal.

Even younger were four boys who had only left school in July 1914. One, Lieutenant Stanley Knight Bates, was commissioned into the King's Own in the autumn of 1914, when he was thought to be the youngest full lieutenant in the British Army. He was killed in action on the Western Front in May 1915, still some weeks short of his eighteenth birthday (his father, Major John H. Bates, second-in-command of the battalion, was wounded at the same time). By then Fred Eltoft and the school porter, Joseph L. Dixon, both of whom had enlisted as privates in the 5th Battalion of the King's Own, were also dead. Eltoft had left the school in 1911, and served an apprenticeship with an engineering firm, while Dixon, aged 33, was a former regular soldier who had re-enlisted on the outbreak of war.

Lieutenant Stanley Knight Bates (WW1photos.com).

Edward Hugh Keir had also left school in the summer of 1914, and been commissioned into the King's Own. He later transferred to the Royal Flying Corps, and was killed in action in 1917, aged 20. The letter from his squadron commander reads:

'I am writing you a few lines just to say how very sad we all are at your son's death. As I expect you know he was attacked in the air today at 3.45 by a German scout, and after putting up a very fine fight he was at last brought down. I have seen his body this evening and he looks quite peaceful and happy, having been killed instantly. His observer, Captain Wasey, was also killed, shot through the heart. It may be some small comfort to you, as it is to me, that he died fighting and suffered no pain. He was a splendid boy, keen and energetic, and a pilot of great promise. He was immensely popular, and I feel that I have lost a personal friend as well as a pilot of great promise. Please accept my deepest sympathy in your great loss.
Yours very sincerely.
C.F.A. Portal.'

This is very much the tone of the letters sent to bereaved relatives, but it is of added interest in that it is signed by Major Charles Portal, who by 1945 was Marshal of the Royal Air Force Lord Portal, Chief of the Air Staff. In 1918 Keir's parents endowed a prize in his memory; this is still awarded annually, currently to a cadets of the RAF Section of the School CCF.

In 1917 Private J.W. Cockcroft of the Civil Service Rifles met his death. He had lived at East Villa (23 East Road, soon to be bought by the school as Storey House, its junior boarding house) and he is commemorated by a stained glass window in Christ Church.

Bates and Keir had been members of the School's 1914 cricket XI, all of whom had volunteered for the army, ten in the early months of the war. Two others (Gunner W.M. Brown and Second Lieutenant N.C. Gornell) also lost their lives, and Private Snowball was listed as missing in 1918, but was later known to have become a prisoner of war. Of the others, Captain A. Bates of the East Lancashire Regiment was awarded the Military Cross, Captain W.H. Metcalfe of the 5th King's Own, the MC and Bar, and Gunner Escolme of the Royal Artillery, the Military Medal.

Although eight members of staff joined the army (at a time when the number of pupils was rising), the governors managed to replace them without having recourse to the unprecedented employment of women teachers. An appeal to the Lancaster tribunal was made in 1918, to defer the call-up for military service of an essential science master, with precedents from Preston and Carlisle cited. Deferment until 31 July was agreed, by which time the necessity was past, as victory was in sight.

In all, over 400 former pupils of the school served, mostly (368) with the army on the Western Front, but twenty-one were with the Royal Navy and eight joined the newly-formed Royal Air Force in 1918, alongside the existing members of the Royal Flying Corps. Three served in the Merchant Navy and one, who had emigrated, with the US Army.

One early volunteer into the Canadian Army was N. Lowden. He had left school in 1902, had graduated in Civil Engineering at London University and, after working in railways in Nigeria, went to Canada in 1909. On his arrival (with the troopship convoy escorted by HMS *Lancaster*), he had been transferred to the Royal Engineers, with whom he won a Military Cross in 1918. This, together with the DSO and MC won by Major H. Gooch, (son of a former headmaster of the National School) also of the Royal Engineers, is now in the school's possession.

CHAPTER 6

Casualties
1916–1918

Conscription had begun in January 1916, but most of the casualties in that year were the earlier volunteers: the new conscripts cannot have been in the trenches before the autumn.

Captain Edward M. Lloyd-Evans of the 5th King's Own was killed in March. A former pupil of the Royal Grammar School, he had enlisted in August 1914, when he was employed as assistant manager at Rembrandt Intaglio Printing Company at Queen's Mill, and had been wounded the previous year. The school has recently added his dress uniform to its archive.

Private John Simpson was serving with the 21st Canadian Regiment when he was killed on 12 June. A former pupil at Skerton School, he had worked at Williamson's before emigrating in 1912. A significant number of former Lancaster men who had emigrated in the years before the war had joined their respective contingents. They included Corporal Charles Bramwell Allen, a former pupil at the Royal Grammar School and son of a previous mayor, who was killed in France when serving with the New Zealand Contingent, and Corporal T.E. Addison, formerly of Primrose Street, who was with the Canadian contingent.

From mid-July the newspapers were filled with the ever-growing casualty lists on the Somme, although both continued to emphasise Allied successes there, at Verdun and on the Middle East and Italian fronts. Probably the first death on the Somme was that of Private George Frederick Ball, a former pupil of the Royal Grammar School, who was one of the almost 20,000 British deaths on 1 July when the offensive began. Lieutenant P.D. Denman of St Oswald Street, and a former pupil of St Thomas's School, also died that day when serving with the Yorkshire Regiment.

Second Lieutenant Joseph Rowley of Havelock Street was killed the next day. He had attended Scotforth School before joining the 1st King's Own and won the DCM as a sergeant major before being commissioned. Another death was that of Lieutenant S. Gooch, son of the former headmaster of the Boys' National School, serving with the King's (Liverpool Regiment).

Two pairs of brothers were among the dead: Sergeant David Nichol of Prospect Street was serving with the Royal Irish Fusiliers. He had attended the National School before working for the grocer T.D. Smith. His brother Private James Nichol, a former pupil of St Thomas's School who had worked for Storeys, was with the 2nd King's Own in Salonika. In July, Lance Corporal J. Cragg, of Gregson Road, serving with the Loyals and in October Private H. Cragg of the King's Own were both killed in action in France. Sadly, these were only the first few of an ever-lengthening list as the weeks went by. They included Lieutenant Colonel C.A.W. Anderson, who had recently taken over command of the 5th Battalion of the King's Own from Lieutenant Colonel Eaves.

In October, however, the Palladium showed the film of the Battle of the Somme, which it described as 'Absolutely the greatest Moving Picture that the world has ever seen, showing the brilliant Victory of the Allies'. There were record houses at each performance (seats cost 6d or 1s) and some of the audience recognised relatives on the screen. The casualty lists featured on a different page!

Photographs of all the Lancaster men were published in the *Guardian*, together with lists of names of the casualties from the King's Own during 1916, and they were featured again in the issue of 30 December. The *Observer* matched this in its first issue of 1917.

Again there were long casualty lists in 1917, when the failure of a French offensive led to the need for Britain's armies to relieve the pressure by an offensive on the Ypres salient, towards the village of Passchendaele. One of those killed here, in November 1917, Gunner

J.T. Curwen of Moor Lane, was serving with the Machine Gun Corps. A former pupil of Bowerham School, and later an employee at Lune Mills, he had already won a Military Medal. Others were Lieutenant S.J. Armstrong, son of the head teacher of Skerton School, serving with the Northumberland Fusiliers, and Lance Corporal J.W. Standen of the Ship Hotel on North Road. He was a former pupil of the Royal Grammar School, and had been working as a teacher in North Shields in 1914, so had enlisted in the Northumberland Fusiliers.

Three other Old Lancastrians fell at this time including Gunner W.M. Brown of the Royal Field Artillery, a former senior prefect and captain of the cricket XI. Captain G. Marriott of the Lancashire Fusiliers had also been senior prefect and then read classics at Peterhouse, Cambridge. He had been teaching at Oldham Grammar School at the outbreak of war. Second Lieutenant W.M. Pinch was teaching at the Boys' National School when he volunteered to join the 5th King's Own.

In March 1918 the Germans launched a major offensive on the Western Front, their forces augmented by a million men transferred from the east after the collapse of Russia. Its initial success was measured in Lancaster by a new rise in casualties, with large numbers of men listed as missing, or as prisoners during the confusion. Among the dead was Private R. Dawson of Tarbet Street, serving with the 5th King's Own, killed on 9 March. He had attended St Peter's School, and was employed at Gillows as a French polisher. Second Lieutenant J. Thompson, formerly of Cavendish Street was educated at Scotforth National School, trained as a teacher, and had become a headmaster by 1914 when he joined the King's Liverpool Regiment.

Major H. Satterthwaite, son of a former mayor was killed on 7 June. He had originally joined the 1st Volunteer Battalion of the King's Own in 1900, serving until 1907. At the outbreak of the war he was a director and assistant manager of the Galgate silk mill, but he immediately rejoined the King's Own, serving in France. In 1917 he was seconded to the Loyal North Lancashire Regiment as its second-in-command.

Second Lieutenant Noel Christopher Gornell of Edith Street, Skerton was killed only a year after leaving school. He won a scholarship from the Boys' National School to the Royal Grammar School, where he was in both the cricket XI and the rugby XV, finally being appointed senior prefect. He was serving with the Royal Engineers.

Among those posted as missing was Second Lieutenant J. Sowerby of Dumbarton Road. A former pupil of St Peter's School, he went on to the Royal Grammar School and then into teaching in Blaydon. He enlisted in the King's Royal Rifles in 1915, was promoted sergeant and then commissioned into the Northumberland Fusiliers. He was subsequently found to be a prisoner of war. Another was Private J.E. Snowball of Meadowside. He attended Bowerham School from where he proceeded to the Royal Grammar School, where he had been in the cricket XI in 1914. He had joined the Welch Regiment, was also listed as missing, and found to have become a prisoner.

The complete text of Field Marshal Haig's famous 'backs to the wall' order to the troops in April 1918 was published in the press to show the seriousness of the situation:

> *'There is no other course open to us but to fight it out. Every position must be held to the last man: there must be no retirement. With our backs to the wall and believing in the justice of our cause each one of us must fight on to the end. The safety of our homes and the Freedom of mankind alike depend upon the conduct of each one of us at this critical moment.'*

However, by the summer it was clear that the German offensive had been held, and a counter offensive was beginning which not only recovered the lost ground, but hustled the Germans out of their main defensive work, the Hindenburg Line. Victory began to look a possibility, but fighting also continued in the Middle East. There Sergeant William Gardner DCM MM of the 2nd King's Own was killed, leaving a widow and seven children at their Bridge Street home.

There were relatively few civilian casualties in this war, but when on 12 September 1918 the Union Castle liner RMS *Galway Castle* was torpedoed by a German submarine en route to Capetown, a Lancaster family was among the 154 lost. Mrs L. Higham was travelling to join her husband in South Africa, together with their three children, Phyllis, aged 9, Leonard (7) and Arthur (5), who had just said goodbye to their friends at Bowerham School.

At the end of September Sergeant John Noon of the Lancashire

Fusiliers, whose wife and child lived at Alexandra Road in Skerton, was killed leading his men in an attack on the German lines during the Allied counter-offensive. He had attended St Peter's School (later known as the Cathedral School) in Balmoral Road, and later was employed at the Lune mills. On the same day, Sergeant Richard Evan Kewley of the King's Own was lost. He had lived in Ullswater Road, attended Christ Church School and then worked at Gillows.

CHAPTER 7

Decorations for Gallantry

Lancaster's first Victoria Cross was won by Second Lieutenant James Edgar Leach, a former pupil of Bowerham School, who was serving with the 2nd Manchester Regiment on the Western Front. The action took place near Festubert on 29 October 1914, when, after their trench had been taken by the Germans and after two attempts at recapture had failed, he and Sergeant John Hogan voluntarily decided to recover the trench themselves. The citation states: 'Working from traverse to traverse at close quarters with great bravery, they gradually succeeded in regaining possession, killing eight of the enemy, wounding two, and making sixteen prisoners.'

James Leach VC – Wikipedia

Another former Lancaster resident to win this highest decoration for gallantry was Lieutenant William Thomas Forshaw, who had taught first at Sulyard Street and then at Dallas Road schools, before moving on to a post at the North Manchester Grammar School. He won his award between 7 and 9 August 1915 when serving with the 6th Manchesters at Gallipoli in 1915 for holding a position against the Turks, throwing bombs for 40 hours, showing 'a fine example and magnificent courage'. The citation also stated: 'When his detachment was relieved, he volunteered to continue directing the defence. Later, when the Turks captured a portion of the trench, he shot three of them and recaptured it. It was due to his fine example and magnificent courage that his very important position was held.'

Eight soldiers of the King's Own won the VC, but none was a native of Lancaster. A report in the *Guardian* in 1917 said that Private J. Foster of Main Street, Skerton had been recommended for the Victoria Cross during the campaign in Mesopotamia, but there is no further reference to this.

On 7 July 1918 the vicar of Hutton Roof (and former headmaster of Bentham Grammar School) the Reverend Theodore

William Thomas Forshaw VC – Wikipedia

Bentham Hardy, who was serving as a chaplain to the forces, was involved in a most heroic rescue under fire. He carried a wounded

Rev T.B. Hardy VC – Wikipedia

officer to safety, and returned to dig out three men who had been buried by a shell explosion 'moving quietly amongst the men and tending the wounded, absolutely regardless of his personal safety'. Already the holder of the DSO and MC, he was now awarded the Victoria Cross. Sadly, in October 1918 as he was attending wounded men in no man's land and, despite being dressed as a padre and unarmed, he was shot by a German sniper. He died of his wounds in Rouen a week later.

There were many winners of the Distinguished Conduct Medal awarded to other ranks. One was Company Sergeant Major J. Hudson of the King's (Liverpool Regiment), a former pupil of Bowerham School, who had then served an apprenticeship as a watchmaker with Rhodes of Penny Street. Another was Sergeant H. Lindsay of the King's Own, a former pupil of Bowerham School who lived in Havelock Street.

A Royal Warrant in 1915 created the Military Cross, intended as a gallantry award for junior officers, leaving the more prestigious Distinguished Service Order principally for majors and above, but it was not until twelve months later that there was an equivalent decoration for men in the ranks – the Military Medal. Company Sergeant Major W. Ball, of Bowerham Road (5th King's Own) was an early recipient of this new award, and was later recommended for the Distinguished Conduct Medal, but was instead awarded a bar to his MM.

Bombardier E.J. Green of Lune Road, and a former pupil of Bowerham School, won his Military Medal with the Royal Field Artillery at the age of 19. Private James Leek of Westham Street, an employee of the White Cross Mill had joined the Duke of Wellington's Regiment and was similarly honoured, as was Sergeant A.S. Thomas of the London Scottish – a former member of the John O'Gaunt Rowing Club. Private H. Scott, son of the local police Superintendent emigrated to Canada in 1913, and enlisted in Princess Patricia's Light Infantry, where he won an Military Medal.

Awarded the Military Cross were Lieutenant R.F. Mansergh of the 7th Manchesters and Captain W. George of the Royal Army Medical Corps, who had served as medical officer to the King's Own. Second Lieutenant R. Riley of the Royal Engineers was a former pupil of Christ Church School, and later on the teaching staff there for four years. Lieutenant G.T.F. Royle of the Royal Artillery was another recipient of the MC; he had been captain of Lancaster Cricket Club.

A former medical officer at the Royal Albert Institution, Captain D.W. Hunter of the Royal Army Medical Corps was awarded the DSO. A most unusual honour was the award of the King of Serbia's silver medal to Air Mechanic G. Hodgson of 14 Squadron, Royal Flying Corps. Living in Seymour Street, he had served an apprenticeship in electrical engineering with the firm of Parkinson in Bulk Street. Why he should be so honoured is not made clear.

Among the honours won by soldiers of the 5th Battalion King's Own, were a CMG (Companion of the Order of St Michael and St George) for Lieutenant Colonel Lord Richard Cavendish of Holker Hall (the first commanding officer), three Distinguished Service Orders, twenty-four Military Crosses (two with bar, and one with two bars), ten Distinguished Conduct Medals, forty-four Military Medals (one with bar) and six Meritorious Service Medals. A commendation from the general went (for undisclosed action) to Corporal H. Dobson of Windermere Road. A former pupil of Christ Church School, he had been the first locally to achieve the King's Scout badge, and enlisted in the 5th King's Own in September 1914.

In June 1916 a large number of awards were announced to men of the 5th Battalion. The DSO was awarded to Lieutenant Colonel F. Eaves of Springfield Terrace, then the commanding officer. Eight awards of the Distinguished Conduct Medal were made, two to Lancaster men, Sergeant O. Price of Dallas Road and Private R. Veevers, a former pupil of the Royal Grammar School. Sergeant W. Ball of Edward Street received the Military Medal, while another DCM went to Private C.H. Smith of the Royal Fusiliers. His father was Mr T.D. Smith, head of the well-known grocery business then in Penny Street.

Those won by Old Lancastrians (former pupils of the Royal Grammar School) include one CB and one CMG, six DSOs (two with bar), fourteen MCs (two with bar), one Distinguished Flying Cross, two Croix de Guerre, five DCMs and four MMs.

The DSO won at Vimy Ridge in June 1916 by Lieutenant Frederick C. Happold for conspicuous gallantry is particularly noteworthy, as this was a decoration not usually given to junior officers – the new Military Cross had been inaugurated for them. It is suggested that it was awarded to signify that he narrowly missed a VC. The citation in the

London Gazette reads: 'For conspicuous gallantry. When the enemy exploded a mine, he at once collected a few men, rushed up and out-bombed a far larger force of the enemy in the crater until reinforcements arrived. After being wounded he continued to lead and encourage his party.' He was also mentioned in despatches in February 1917.

Frederick Happold left the school in 1912, and had completed two years of a history degree at Peterhouse, Cambridge when the war began. He immediately volunteered, joining the King's Own, but was commissioned into the North Lancashire Regiment (the Loyals). After the war, he returned to Cambridge, completed his degree and a teaching qualification, and later served for thirty years as headmaster of Bishop Wordsworth's School, Salisbury. During the Second World War he served as an officer in the Training Branch of the Royal Air Force. He

A portrait of Frederick C. Happold DSO courtesy of Bishop Wordsworth's School, Salisbury where he was headmaster.

was well known in academic circles for his books on education and religion. He died in 1971.

Engine Room Artificer G.H.F. McCarten, serving in HMS *Invincible*, won the navy's Distinguished Service Medal at the Battle of the Falkland Islands. A former pupil of St Peter's School, he had been an engineering apprentice at the Phoenix Foundry before entering the navy in 1899. Sadly he lost his life when *Invincible* was sunk at Jutland with all her crew. His fellow ERA David Wilson of Blades Street went down in the sister ship *Indefatigable*.

The rare Edward Medal was awarded to four of the rescuers after the explosion of the White Lund munitions factory in 1917. One of these, awarded to police sergeant Thomas Coppard was, in November 2014, acquired for the City Museum's permanent collection, which also features the medals of the Order of the British Empire awarded to foreman Charles Taylor and telephonist Mary Wilkinson. (More on the factory explosion in Chapter 8)

In late 1917 five more Lancaster men were awarded the Military Medal. Private A. Pattison of Willow Lane, who attended St Mary's School and then worked for the Post Office, was in the Royal Army Medical Corps, serving with 20 Field Ambulance. Lance Corporal G. Mawson of Queen Street was with the King's Own at Ypres. After leaving Sulyard Street School he was employed at Williamson's Greenfield Mill. Two former Ripley pupils similarly honoured were Private J. Emmott of the East Lancashires and Sergeant T. Smith of the West Yorkshires, as was Sapper E.B. Rawlinson, formerly of St Thomas's School.

A recipient of the DCM was Corporal W. Fuller of Dalton Square, serving with the King's Scottish Light Infantry. A former pupil of Bowerham School, he had been employed at Williamson's.

The Military Cross was awarded to two Old Lancastrians, Captain A. Bates of the East Lancashires and Captain J. Hunter of the King's (Liverpool Regiment). After leaving the Royal Grammar School in 1902, he played for, and captained the Lancashire Rugby Union team for several seasons. He enlisted at the outbreak of war and was wounded in 1916.

Of the 5th King's Own, Second Lieutenant Ronald Macdonald of Fern Bank, a former pupil of the Friends' School, was awarded the MC in 1917 and a bar to it, and then a second bar in the following year, in each case 'for conspicuous gallantry and devotion to duty'. The citation for the second bar states: 'He went continually to and fro from Brigade Headquarters under very heavy shell fire, bringing most valuable intelligence, and although blown down several times by the shelling which killed and wounded a number of men, he stayed by them, tied up their wounds, and carried several of them to aid posts. His conduct was beyond all praise.'

Captain C.A. Hinton of Scotforth attended Bowerham School and was then articled to the architects Austin & Paley before joining the Royal Engineers, with whom he won the MC.

Private E.C. Nicholls, of the King's Own, formerly a pupil at the National School and later a dental mechanic, received the MM, while a Serbian Silver Medal was awarded to Private W. Whitbread of Bradshaw Street, serving with the Royal Army Medical Corps.

In 1918 the parents of Sergeant W. Grime of the King's Own Scottish Borderers were notified of his Military Medal and, in the same week, were told that his younger brother, Private Joseph Grime of the Grenadier Guards, was missing in action during the German Spring Offensive.

In May 1918 two former pupils were presented with their decorations at a ceremony at Bowerham School. They were Sergeant B.E. Hall of the King's Own Scottish Borderers who had been awarded the Distinguished Conduct Medal, and Driver E. Watson of the Royal Field Artillery who received the Military Medal.

Little is recorded of Lancaster women serving as nurses, but in early 1918 Miss F.M. Hall of Portland Street, matron of a hospital on the Balkan front, and Miss Henrietta Foster were among those honoured with awards from the Red Cross.

CHAPTER 8

The Home Front 1916–1918

One of the earliest events of 1916 was a tea party and concert given by Mr H.G. Storey for the widows and children of soldiers killed in action. It was held in the Drill Hall in Phoenix Street, and the *Guardian* published a lengthy and moving account written by the volunteer who had visited the homes to distribute the tickets.

A happier event was the marriage of Lieutenant James E. Leach VC, who, with his bride, was shortly afterwards the guest at a reception by the Mayor. He was presented with an illuminated address congratulating him on the award, and, as a wedding present, an antique silver tea service. A concert followed, with the band of the 2nd Battalion King's Own and a number of vocalists, and the next day he visited his old school at Bowerham. Sadly, his new wife died just four months after the wedding, aged only 19, and he himself was invalided out of front line duties shortly afterwards.

The new year opened with the usual entertainments on offer. At the Grand Theatre there was 'an intensely funny revue', entitled 'Would You Believe It?', featuring 'the eight Calais girls in chic terpsichorean exhibitions'. The Picturedrome was showing 'a very fine picture "How Callahan Cleaned Up Little Hell"', Callahan being a New York cop sent to an area of the city which was riddled with crime and vice. At the Palladium, Hippodrome and Co-operative Hall were equally unmissable programmes.

The passage of the Military Service Act in February 1916 necessitated the appointment of a tribunal to hear cases, and the initial response was to reappoint that which had been brought into existence by the National Registration scheme, with two additional members to ensure that a quorum would always be available. They were soon busy, hearing requests both by individuals and their employers for exemption from military service for those who claimed that they were doing essential war work. The local solicitors Mr J.S. Oglethorpe and Mr T.P. Tilly were in regular attendance to represent the appellants, but in 1918 a new government regulation ended this practice.

WHO CAN CLAIM EXEMPTION? enquired the *Observer*.

'No man having physical and mental ability to serve in the fighting, or the munitions industry. All such are wanted, and it is a fact that all may be insufficient to finish the war quickly. No male person can claim to be outside of this awful calamity that has befallen the peace-making nations. Our Radicals, Liberals and Labourites have, by their political opinions powerfully helped Prussian designs. The time has gone for any exemptions from civil duties. The country needs every available man, and it is the duty of the local tribunals to see that every man of military age, who is medically fit, undertakes duty for King and Country. Neither religious scruples, social position or business obligations can exempt a man. Yet there are those pleading at the tribunals for exemption for themselves or their servants. What will be their position? They will be social lepers, abhorred and shamed as cowards.'

The tribunals had no such over-riding assumptions, but were required to hear each case and decide on its merits. On one morning in February, eleven pleas were heard. One was from a dentist, who pointed out that his partner was already serving. He was supported by Colonel Duffin of Bowerham Barracks, who said that the man was doing essential dentistry for the soldiers under his command. This secured his exemption for as long as he continued to do such work.

An architect, whose partner was already at the front, was supervising the building of new houses and was granted three months exemption, but a grocer who claimed that his contract for feeding the 'munitioneers' at White Lund required the services of his assistant, was refused.

This was a not unusual balance: when thirty-three appeals were heard on one day in March, six were allowed, fifteen dismissed, seven granted temporary exemption and the rest were deferred. Those refused included a bank official, a grocer's assistant and a scrap metal dealer, all with very plausible claims against which the tribunal hardened its collective heart. Temporary exemptions, usually for three months, were given to a market gardener, a boot salesman, an ironmonger's assistant and a farm worker.

On another day eleven applications were heard from conscientious objectors who claimed exemption on religious or moral grounds. All were closely examined, and the decisions deferred until all had been heard. The outcome was that nine were accepted, including that of a man who had declared his willingness to enlist in the Friends' Ambulance Service. Another was a master at the Friends' School, the Society of Friends having been firmly established in Lancaster since the late seventeenth century. The *Observer*, of course, had its say:

> *'Conscientious Objectors (so-called) are not receiving much sympathy, either from the tribunals or the public – and certainly not from the married men who have attested and who were led to believe that all single men would be called up first. The men who appear before tribunals and apply for exemption on moral and religious grounds are not looked upon as martyrs or as men contending for a vital principle. Rather are they suspected of trying to shelter themselves behind a phrase, especially those whose previous words and actions show that they are animated by self-interest rather than by service, sacrifice or love of country.'*

In fact the tribunal regularly showed sympathy towards members of the Society of Friends – the Quakers – especially to those willing to undertake non-combatant roles. Appellants claiming domestic reasons (often the support of an aged mother) were rarely successful. One successful appeal was for a tram driver and a fitter, whose work was claimed to be essential for the running of the service. The military representative claimed that the tramway was a 'luxury', as the distances to Scotforth and Moorlands were short, and that people could walk. The tribunal did not agree. During the hearing it became apparent that youths of below military age were being employed as conductors and that the numbers of passengers, and hence the revenues, were both increasing.

In November new government guidelines for the tribunals emphasised the urgent need for skilled men in areas of work of importance for the war effort, and such applications were allowed. A special session of the Tribunal was held in February 1917 to consider the effect of conscription on Lancaster industry, looking specifically at the cases of 103 men employed at Williamson's, and thirty-eight at Storeys. Lord Ashton, owner of Williamson's pointed out that he had already lost fifty-eight per cent of his workforce, and the loss of so many more would lead to the closure of Lune Mills, and the loss of employment for about 2,500 workers, almost 600 of them women and girls. The military representative had called for a review, contending that the army needed more men, and questioning whether the work could be said to be essential to the war effort. After a good deal of discussion, it was decided to extend exemption to 31 March, a decision upheld when the military authority made an appeal. At that point came the revelation that the Williamson's workforce had reduced from 3,585 men in 1914 to 1,269 and, while women were being employed in place of some men, 'their power to do the work of men in a linoleum factory is limited'. The danger of the works having to be closed down was, for the moment averted, but 'there is an irreducible minimum with which the work can carry on', and this remained a matter of concern for the rest of the war.

A case was held before the magistrates in March 1917 when the brothers G.M. and T.M. Kelsall were charged with failing to comply with a military order, and their father with aiding and abetting them. They had been called for medical examination to ascertain their fitness for military service, but had replied by letter saying that as long-standing members of the Society of Friends they could not in conscience comply. It was pointed out to the court that two other brothers were already in France serving with the Friends' Ambulance service. Each was fined ten shillings, though the maximum fine was £100 and six months imprisonment.

Those involved in agriculture were much to the fore, and the tribunal soon drew up guidelines for itself, differentiating between those in full time farm work and occasional labourers. A frequent claim was that farmers often allowed their hired labourers to go, while claiming exemption for their sons. The most sympathetic outcome was often deferment of call-up for a few months, often until the harvest was in. On one occasion the chairman exclaimed, 'I warned you farmers that this tribunal is here to get men into the army, and not to let them off.' No doubt those appealing thought otherwise.

Another meeting in May heard an appeal on behalf of a butcher's slaughterman, resulting in a stay of call-up for four weeks to allow the town's butchers to co-operate and enable some men to be released. An exemption granted to a man, conditional on his employment, was cancelled when it was found that he had changed jobs, while other applications on behalf of a baker, a bank employee, a tailor, a gardener and a joiner were refused. In six other cases a temporary exemption of up to three months was allowed. Of thirty-three cases heard on a single day in July, all but three resulted in a temporary exemption of a few months, although this really only deferred the decision, as the men would certainly apply again.

Often such exemptions were linked with an obligation to join the Voluntary Training Corps, whose activities in providing rudimentary military training had been reported from time to time. In late 1916 its members took over the duty of guarding railway lines. Also increasingly active was the Cadet Battalion of the King's Own. Its formation had been suggested by the Mayor in September 1914, and it had been formed the following February, but had not been very much reported. In March 1916 it held a route march to Halton and back, after a church parade at the Priory Church, and in April a photograph of five officers and 70 cadets was published. The unit, under its commanding officer, Lieutenant Colonel Thorn, was inspected the following year. The inspecting officer commented not only on the high standard of the drill and physical fitness demonstration, but also on the cadet NCOs who had been in charge.

The contingent of the Officers' Training Corps at Lancaster Royal Grammar School also continued to train and a new rifle range was opened by the school's games field. It was an open range, with butts simply constructed of railway sleepers, but had the approval of the War Office, though it would be well short of today's safety standards. It was

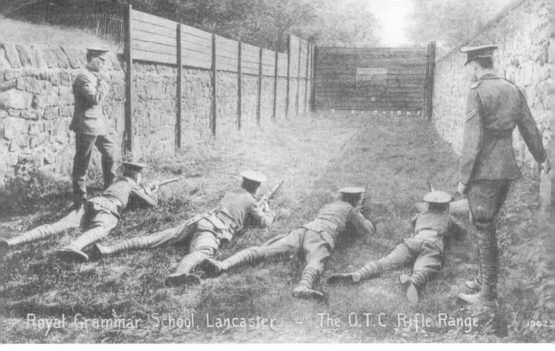

OTC Rifle-Range (LRGS)

opened on Empire Day (24 May) 1917, with the Mayor and the Town Clerk firing the first shots.

The month of March 1916 brought severe weather conditions to Lancaster. Snow fell, then melted resulting in floods and there were gales. This disrupted telephone and telegraph communications, despite the work of men of the Royal Engineers to assist their civilian counterparts. Rail services, especially on the main line to London were unreliable, with trains running late or not at all. Spring arrived in early April with sunshine and rising temperatures. With this came the Quarter Sessions, where there was only one criminal charge to be heard and, as the accused pleaded guilty, there was no case to be heard before a jury. This caused some comment, as sixty men had been summoned for jury service, quite unnecessarily.

The passage into law of the Summer Time Bill was described as 'an interesting and novel event', with the railways and the post office obliged to observe 'clock time', though this was not binding on individuals, and the innovation was regarded as a purely wartime measure. When it came to an end in October, it was hailed as 'an unqualified success', with the confident expectation that it would be implemented again in the following year. In October, schools were encouraged to shorten the 'midday vacation' to enable them to close an hour earlier. Not only would this lead to savings in coal (most classrooms were still heated by open fires) and lighting, but would allow children to reach home in daylight. Shops were also urged to close an hour earlier, for the same reason, and churches to reschedule their Sunday evening services to the afternoon. In fact an amendment to DORA made compulsory the closing of shops at 7pm on weekdays, 8pm on Fridays and 9pm on Saturdays from 6 October.

In April 1916 the government announced the formation of a Non-Combatant Corps, to be filled by those conscientious objectors willing to serve as (for example) stretcher-bearers or ambulance drivers. This again aroused the *Lancaster Observer* to denounce these *'invincible conscientious objectors, supported by the "Asquitheans" in the government'*. (Mr Asquith was soon to be replaced as Prime Minister by David Lloyd George, currently Minister for Munitions.) The paper launched a parallel attack on the 'Clyde anarchists' – shipbuilding workers who had gone on strike. At the time the Easter Rising in Dublin had given rise to headlines such as CIVIL WAR IN DUBLIN and WHO SHALL RULE IRELAND?

The tribunal continued to meet weekly and in January 1918 the military representative challenged 132 exemptions which had been allowed, on the basis of the needs of local industries. A decision on the appeal was deferred, and exemption was eventually allowed up to 31 August, by which time the war was almost won. For the rest of the year the majority of appellants were allowed temporary exemption, which in practice meant that they did not serve.

A shortage of newsprint led to the announcement that the local newspapers would be produced only to order, with no surplus copies, and in the same issue was a report (with photograph) of the Scouts and members of the Church Lads' Brigade who had collected 42 tons of old newspapers, valued for scrap at £116. Both newspapers continued to run their advertisement columns, with the conventional publicity from well-established firms varied by two from Hunters – 'Munition workers should try Hunter's men's overalls' and 'Women munition workers – sleeved overalls and caps, ready-made, or made to order'.

In August an official list was published of the names and last known addresses of 124 men (fifty-seven from Lancaster itself) who had failed to report to the Recruiting Officer in Lancaster after being sent call-up papers. Information on their whereabouts was urgently sought. A week later there was a correction: the whereabouts of eighty-three of these men was known (many of them granted permanent or temporary exemption by the tribunals), while sixteen were already serving in the army!

The trades unions had opposed conscription from the start, and at a meeting at the King's Arms in Lancaster of the Miners' Federation of Great Britain, a resolution was passed calling for the repeal of the Act, and for concerted action to be taken with other unions to achieve this. 'It is resolved that the conference expresses its opposition to the spirit of conscription, and determines to exercise a vigilant scrutiny of any proposed extension to the Military Service Act.'

The further restrictions, under DORA, on lighting were, it was claimed, causing hardship and inconvenience early in 1916, when shops were required to close earlier, and when there were numerous cases in the courts for non-compliance. A shopkeeper of Meeting House Lane, whose premises had been 'brilliantly illuminated' was fined £5 with the alternative of twenty-eight days imprisonment, while a grocer was similarly punished for breaking the restrictions on the sale of alcohol. The Master of the Workhouse was fined 5s for a lighted window, and the Headmaster of the Royal Grammar School was similarly penalised when a junior boarder left a light on.

Characteristically, the *Lancaster Observer* came out with wholehearted support for the restrictions. On the closure of footpaths and bridges it had this to say:

> *'The sharp challenge of sentries, and the gleam of steel as a fixed bayonet confronts a pedestrian is alarming, but happily no awkward event has taken place. It should be recognised that sentries stationed at different places are not there for spectacular purposes but for stern business. It would be of little use if they were not so empowered.'*

Some of these duties were being carried out by the members of the Voluntary Training Corps, which had received a favourable report on its first inspection, once the War Office had given the organisation its formal approval. 'Such a defence corps is admirable in every way. It is an example on the part of men past military age to young men in the heyday of their lives, and has given facilities for these young men to obtain preliminary training.'

Despite all of the foregoing, it is clear that the policy of 'business as usual' continued to be invoked. While the Battle of the Somme was claiming lives, there are reports of cricket, swimming and bowls matches, and the cinemas continued to show films. (These were the Hippodrome in Dalton Square, now the City Architect's office, the Palladium in Market Street, now W.H. Smiths, the Picturedrome in Lower Church Street and the Empire, in the Co-operative Hall). At the Grand Theatre Mr Charles Brandon's repertory company was staging Sheridan's 'School for Scandal', while Irelands of Chapel Street advertised that their 'chars-a-banc departed daily for Blackpool and the Lakes'. The situations vacant columns were full of the usual job opportunities and the shops were advertising their wares.

A garden fete on the Lune Road ground of Lancaster Cricket Club raised over £500 in aid of disabled soldiers and sailors. A more sombre note was struck by the report of a boating disaster in the Lune estuary off Cockersands Abbey. A boat capsized, and seven of the eight young Lancaster men on board drowned. Only one was a strong enough swimmer to make the shore, and he was the main witness at the subsequent inquest.

The Council remained active in dealing with the day to day running of the town, and in March 1916 its budget imposed substantial increases in gas and electricity prices (both then controlled locally) while a recommendation for the purchase of a motor ambulance at a cost of £315 was approved. Plans for the widening and resurfacing of Caton Road were also made, with foundations strong enough to bear the expected heavy traffic. (Much of this was due to the munitions factory, though this was not referred to openly.)

In March the death of the veteran solicitor Mr W. Tilly was reported. He had been a pupil at Lancaster Royal Grammar School, had served for some years as a councillor, but since 1902, when the borough of Morecambe was instituted, had been its Town Clerk. His funeral was at Morecambe Parish Church. Soon afterwards came the death, at 85, of Mr E.B. Dawson of Aldcliffe Hall. He was a barrister on the Northern Circuit who had also for many years been a Justice of the Peace, chairman of the Quarter Sessions, a Deputy Lieutenant and Constable of Lancaster Castle. His funeral, at the Centenary

Congregational Church at Stonewell, saw a church packed with representatives of all branches of the town's society. And then came the death of Canon Billington, Rector of St Peter's Roman Catholic Church (not yet a cathedral). He had held that post for twenty-two years, during which he had been responsible for the building of the baptistry and the establishment of St Joseph's Church at Skerton and its school.

Not only were the annual meetings of the Co-operative Congress and the Oddfellows held in Lancaster at Whitsuntide, but the Educational Handwork Association met in the town, which made 'Lancaster more and more a conference town. The facilities offered by the corporation are very much on the right lines, and visitors should leave Lancaster with pleasant memories because of the courtesy and hospitality of the people.'

From 16–22 July 1916 was designated War Savings Week nationwide. The populace was encouraged to:

Save labour – everybody can help

- Cut down your meat bill
- Reduce the amount of gas, electricity and coal you use
- Do not ask the shopkeeper to deliver small parcels – take them home yourself
- Give a regular order for your newspaper instead of buying it haphazard, and thus avoid waste of paper and labour
- Every little helps, and if everyone will economise wherever and whenever possible, much will be done.
- Save money also. During the week every man woman and child in the country should start to do something definite in the way of lending money to their country. By Saturday, everyone should be able to show some definite proof of what he or she has lent to help to win the war.
- What will YOU have to show?

There followed instructions on how to form a War Savings Association in workplaces and schools.

The various sub-committees continued to operate, while in November the energetic Mayor, Councillor W. Briggs, was re-elected

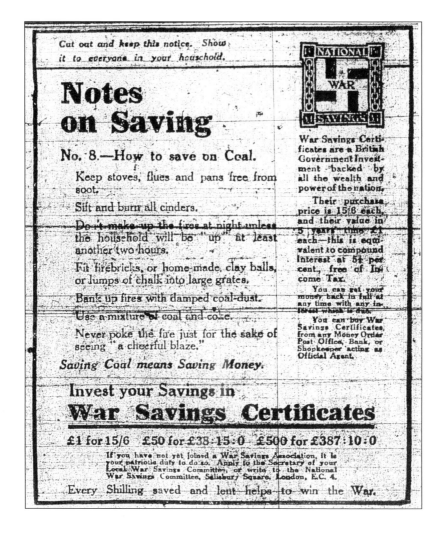

Cut out and keep this notice. Show it to everyone in your household.

Notes on Saving

No. 8.—How to save on Coal.

Keep stoves, flues and pans free from soot.

Sift and burn all cinders.

Don't make up the fires at night unless the household will be "up" at least another two hours.

Fit firebricks, or home-made clay balls, or lumps of chalk into large grates.

Bank up fires with damped coal-dust.

Use a mixture of coal and coke.

Never poke the fire just for the sake of seeing "a cheerful blaze."

Saving Coal means Saving Money.

War Savings Certificates are a British Government Investment backed by all the wealth and power of the nation.

Their purchase price is 15/6 each, and their value in 5 years' time £1 each—this is equivalent to compound Interest at 5½ per cent, free of Income Tax.

You can get your money back in full at any time with any interest when it is due.

You can buy War Savings Certificates from any Money Order Post Office, Bank, or Shopkeeper acting as Official Agent.

Invest your Savings in
War Savings Certificates

£1 for 15/6   £50 for £38:15:0   £500 for £387:10:0

If you have not yet joined a War Savings Association, it is your patriotic duty to do so. Apply to the Secretary of your Local War Savings Committee, or write to the National War Savings Committee, Salisbury Square, London, E.C. 4.

Every Shilling saved and lent helps to win the War.

for a fourth term. By then he was not only presiding at council meetings and sitting as a magistrate, but was chairman of the Water Committee. A major concern was the improvement in the water supply for the town and an ambitious scheme was proposed, which would, however, be costly. An increase of twenty-five per cent in the water rate was estimated to add a shilling in the pound to the domestic rates.

One innovation in late 1917 was the purchase of three electric motor-buses. The first to be delivered was employed on a route from

Lancaster to Skerton, but this met with some criticism and even ridicule at first. The inhabitants of Skerton claimed that whenever they wanted to travel into Lancaster, 'the 'bus was going in the opposite direction' – and vice versa, of course. It was not yet clear what routes would be followed by the other two when they were delivered – the electric tramway had for a dozen years been plying its services elsewhere – to Moorlands and Scotforth for example. Three months later the venture was hailed as a great, profit-making success. A new route took the munitions workers to the Caton Road factory and two more vehicles had been ordered. It was decided to borrow the considerable sum of £6,000 to expand the service further, with routes to Marsh and Freehold, as 'the successes of the service are marked. They have proved a great boon to residents generally, and to workers in particular.'

The possibility that this might lead to a reduction in the tramway was raised. The Tramway Committee was under pressure late in 1917 when the price of electricity was raised by twenty-five per cent, which added to the burden on householders and traders. Gas was still used more than electricity, especially for lighting and cooking, and the gas company was making good progress despite the rising price of coal. A

Electric 'buses in Market Square (LCM).

A Lancaster Tram (LCM)

suggestion was made that the water resources might be utilised to provide hydro-electricity, but this could only have been a solution in the long term. In 1918, however, the tramway seemed secure, offering a penny fare from the Market to Scotforth or Bowerham, or a sixpenny fare to Morecambe, with stages en route. Boys were employed as conductors, though their exuberance in changing over the connector to the overhead cables caused some adverse comment, and the suggestion was even made that women might be employed! 'We hope they will prove to the Committee that they can perform the duties to the satisfaction of the public and their employers. We feel certain that they will receive the support of the Committee if they are determined to carry out their duties in an able and courteous way.'

Petrol too was in short supply. While the country could produce a fair proportion of the food it needed, it was entirely dependent on imports of oil and the losses of tankers to submarines was continuing. Not only were supplies reduced, but the demands of the services were increasing. As a result, the use of motor cars (as they were still known) for pleasure came to an end and attempts were made to reduce the demands for trade. Commercial deliveries had to be reduced in number and attempts were made to get retailers to co-operate in deliveries out of town.

In December 1916 a municipal census was held, partly to support the application for Lancaster to be designated a County Borough, with an increase in its responsibilities. It had, as a subsidiary aim, the compilation of a roll of honour of all Lancaster men serving with the colours – thought to number about 5,000. There was also a bid for city status (not conceded until 1937), and for the title of Lord Mayor, but this was unsuccessful.

The first event of 1917 was the annual treat for some 800 old folk, given by Mr H.L. Storey, but the year opened otherwise with very restricted railway services, and the prohibition of the sale of white flour.

In May 1917 the town was honoured by a visit from the King George V and Queen Mary. A route was organised to enable as many as possible to see and cheer the royal couple in their car. They passed along St Leonardgate, where the workers of Gillows were in attendance, and then along Caton Road where there was a large assembly of schoolchildren. They then toured *'the huge government engineering works – one of the largest in the country'*. Here the reports

Royal visit (LCM)

in the *Observer* have a distinctly censored look, with the word 'munitions' implicit, but never mentioned, though *'the many processes and operations for the manufacture of weapons of war'* included a reference to the turning of 6-inch and 9.2-inch naval shells (leaving little to the imagination).

> *'Their Majesties spent much time in the works, and their inspection of the various processes, the interest they showed in the workers, their conversations with them, and their graciousness throughout gave unbounded satisfaction.'*

The members of the managerial staff were introduced, a woman worker presented a bouquet to the Queen, and, most bizarrely, there was *'an impressive march past of the huge mobile cranes'*.

The *Guardian*, on the other hand, was much freer in its report, identifying the projectile works by name, and also describing the subsequent visit to the shell filling factory at White Lund.

Later in the year a hostel for the women workers was built by the Girls' Friendly Society, and the YMCA premises on China Street became a social centre. Wages were raised to 2/6 per hour for women over 18, and to 1/3 for those under 18. (Women comprised some three-quarters of the workforce). In May of 1917 the National Projectile Vaudeville Society staged an entertainment at the Hippodrome, in aid of the Royal Lancaster Infirmary's funds. It was 'bright and interesting throughout, excellently staged, interspersed with charming dances and effective choruses and full of bright humour.' Its three productions raised £100 for the RLI.

That summer also saw the men of the factory in a cricket league, with ten teams competing, including the Tool Room, Millwrights, the Six Inch (shell) Department and the Sixty Pounders. The scores were published week by week. There followed the formation of a football league, with the men and ladies of the Lancaster factory competing against their counterparts in Barrow and elsewhere. The Amateur Operatic and Dramatic Society staged a concert in aid of the YMCA Hut, with a male voice quartet, violin solos, solo dances and duets, and 'a really excellent pierrot entertainment by the High Explosives'.

Then in February 1918 a fancy dress ball was held at the Projectiles Club in Gage Street, with over 300 attending, half of them in fancy dress. Historical, humorous rural and military costumes included a Quaker girl, a farmer's boy, a Swedish peasant, a French pierrot, nigger (sic) minstrels, Red Cross nurses, Charles II and Nell Gwynne. The prizewinners were a woman worker dressed as 'Vive la France' and a man representing Uncle Sam – tactful bows to our old and new allies in the present war.

Later a juvenile fancy dress ball was held at the Phoenix Rooms, in aid of St Dunstan's Hospital for blinded servicemen. Girls appeared as Belgian soldiers, a witch, Red Cross nurses and Cleopatra, with boys dressed as a huntsman, a monk, jesters and a jockey. The NPFL Operatic and Dramatic Society then staged 'The Dairymaids' to large and enthusiastic audiences, in aid of the Prisoners of War relief fund; to this production wounded soldiers were admitted free of charge.

The munitions court continued to publish cases where employees (mostly male) were found to have tobacco, cigarettes and matches in their possession, and to punish them with prison sentences involving hard labour, but this does not seem to have been an effective deterrent.

By 1918 heavier fines were being imposed, including two of 40s (£2) for men who had lost, respectively 110 hours over a two month period and 166 hours in three months. Each was earning over £3 per week. Another was fined £3 for sleeping on duty. The hazards of the work were underlined by a number of inquests following fatal accidents, one involving a young woman hit by a shell case which had slipped out of its sling, suspended beneath a travelling crane and in another case, a death from an industrial disease.

The opticians department of Leightons ran a series of advertisements aimed at the munitions workers. The first read:

'Look to your eyes. The girl munitions worker who spends hours working by artificial light finds that she becomes troubled by "eye weariness" – just a slight smarting that is usually passed by, but which, if neglected may develop into something more serious.'

Mr Leighton would give helpful advice and, if necessary, supply glasses which would deal with the problem.

A fete in aid of the fund to provide food parcels for prisoners of war was organised in the summer of 1917 by the local branch of the National Federation of Women Workers. It was held at Bailrigg, then the home of Mr and Mrs H.L. Storey, whose gardens and terraces were open to the public, and it was extensively reported in the *Observer*. A fine sunny June day enabled 'ample and varied entertainments, with the band of the King's Own Royal Lancaster Regiment in attendance. Dancing on the greensward was a popular pastime, and there was much gaiety and merriment.' A large number of wounded soldiers from the military hospitals at Wray, Heysham and Bowerham were also present, and £1,400 was raised.

A similar, but smaller scale event was held in the following week at the Lune Road cricket ground, but on that occasion the weather was less kind. A fete at Ellel Grange raised £300 for St Dunstan's Hostel for blinded sailors and soldiers, while in December a Christmas gift sale organised by the Mayoress raised £700 for the same cause.

The annual prize-giving at the Girls' Grammar School in February 1917 gives an indication of the role of former pupils in the war. The headmistress, Miss Phillimore, said that 'old girls are doing useful work on the railways, in post offices, banks and munitions factories and on farms and in gardens'. At the same time there was mention of a Miss Doris Cliff of the Lancaster St John's Ambulance Brigade, who had been working for two years in the East Leeds Military Hospital.

However, the use of women workers in new areas was still somewhat controversial. Lancaster does not seem to have any 'omnibus conductorettes' found in some major cities. At the end of 1917 the *Observer* summarised matters in these words:

> '*Women have done splendidly, according to their abilities, but there are some occupations that women cannot undertake. But the female industrial army that has been created is a modern miracle. Women are backing up the men splendidly and the comradeship and mutual respect which is growing is in every way commendable. There are some things to deplore, no doubt, but generally the co-operation of the sexes has worked splendidly.*'

At the Vestry meeting of the Parish Church at Easter 1918, it was announced that 'ladies have invaded the belfry', taking the places of men who had been called for military service. 'There is no sphere in which the war has not brought women, and they have proved themselves capable substitutes, even in the ringing of church bells.' At the same time the new constitution of the Conservative Association opened all positions to women.

At the Petty Sessions there was what was described as 'a disquieting case'. Two young boys were charged with breaking into a lock-up shop, one keeping watch while the other broke in. They stole two rifles, which they kept for some weeks until discovered. Again the lack of fatherly control was blamed. Another case involved two boys, of fifteen and ten who had entered Gorrill's shop one Sunday, and had stolen £1 6s 6d from the till. The younger boy was sentenced to receive six strokes of the birch, while the elder, who had already received this punishment for a previous offence, was fined £3. Later cases involved the activities of an organised gang, the thefts of a bicycle, two wrist watches and vegetables from allotments.

Another matter of increasing concern was the supply of food. Councillors urged that land be made available in John o'Gaunt ward for allotments, and one suggested that the park would be better used for growing potatoes rather than flowers. The *Observer* was later to comment:

> '*Allotment holders are playing the part of silent heroes. Some have taken up plots on the Greaves estate which, up to a few days ago, formed a common playground – hard, stony, derelict land which held no promise at all. Yet, with wonderful patience and persistent labour, the debris has been cleared, the rough stones removed and the soil broken up and made the most of. In normal times such a plot would not have been worth the labour of its clearing and working. But the men who have tackled the job are British, and they realise that there is a need, they have faced the task and carried it out, and are going to make the unpromising bit of earth yield its increase. If these allotment holders receive no material award, they will receive a better reward – they will know that they have helped to save their country.*'

By the summer of 1918 there were schoolboy plots available at Skerton being tended by boys aged ten to fourteen years of age.

The shortage of sugar had inhibited Lancaster housewives from their usual jam-making in 1917, and in the following March an official announcement stated that 'cane sugar is not necessary to the maintenance of health and strength. Before the advent of (imported) cane sugar people lived healthy lives. There are other forms of sugar which are just as suitable – honey, jam and marmalade and milk sugar and the sugar found in vegetables such as beetroot, parsnips, carrots and onions, and in fresh, dried, tinned and bottled fruits.' It is not recorded how the jam might be made without sugar, nor the marmalade without imported oranges or lemons.

Early in 1917 an acute shortage of potatoes was reported. Normally, local supplies were supplemented by potatoes imported from Ireland, but these imports had been banned 'nobody knows why', and it was thought that local farmers were withholding stocks, in the hopes of a rise in prices. With the imposition of the unrestricted submarine campaign by Germany food shortages became more serious, and there was 'a growing feeling that the compulsory rationing of certain foodstuffs is imperative if we are to effect sufficient economy in the consumption of food to tide us over the dangerous period of threatened shortage for which the German submarine campaign is responsible.'

A voluntary food restriction scheme operated from February 1917. Each person was to be limited to four pounds of bread, two and a half pounds of meat and three quarters of a pound of sugar per week. This would not be enforced by officials – it was 'honour-based' compliance, and was backed up by much advice on how to make the best use of what was available. Meat should be stewed, not roasted, and the stock reserved for a second dish. Good use of a variety of vegetables was encouraged, but the real issue was the acute shortage of wheat. Oatmeal, rice, lentils, barley and beans should be used to the utmost, with economy a major factor. 'If everyone ate a pound of bread less per week than at present, the threatened famine would be averted.'

The return of bad weather compounded the problem. As in 1916, snow and frost at the end of March and in early April meant that 'everything is very backward. Trees show little sign of foliage, vegetation is at a standstill, ploughing is only carried out with difficulty, and seedbeds are almost impossible because of the saturated soil.'

The stock of potatoes was almost exhausted, and turnips and carrots were becoming scarce, with a consequent rise in prices.

A Food Hoarding Order required that 'no person shall after 9 April 1917 acquire any article of food which exceeds the quantity required for ordinary use in the household'. A voluntary rationing of bread to four pounds per week was a first stage, but this was swiftly followed by elaborate restrictions on hotels, boarding houses, restaurants and teashops. These limited the amount of meat in any dish (with Tuesdays to be meatless days in London, and Wednesdays elsewhere) and with a ban on potatoes, except on meatless days. Teashops were similarly restricted, with many varieties of cake prohibited, to conserve sugar. One result not anticipated was the appearance of bogus food inspectors who used the pretext of a search for illicitly-hoarded foodstuffs for theft. Householders were advised that genuine inspectors would have written authority and be accompanied by a police officer.

Regular columns on 'Food and how to save it' were written 'at the request of the Food Controller', and in early 1917 there was a series of demonstrations in the lecture hall of the Storey Institute by a senior domestic science teacher on making appetising dishes. Four recipes using sheeps' heads were published. These involved making Scotch barley broth, boiling the bones to make stock, and poaching the brains and simmering the tongue in the stock. A further recipe showed how to make a fish pie from a cod's head. The course was so popular that it had to be repeated. Another tip was to augment butter by mixing with an equal amount of cornflour and milk, while in an age before domestic refrigerators there was advice on 'how to make the most of milk', which should be covered and kept cool. Housewives were advised that 'no bacon is too fat: the chief value lies in the fat which is essential to energy'. Dried fruits were scarce, as the troops had the first call, but by the autumn blackberries were plentiful.

By 1917 there were shortages of margarine and tea, with complaints that there was some unfairness in food distribution, and a formal system of rationing was the answer. The Council was required to appoint a Food Control Committee of up to twelve members. Chaired by the tireless Mayor, it had to include at least one representative of labour and one lady. Six councillors were nominated together with two members of the Co-operative movement, to represent the retailers, a union representative, and a Miss Oliver as the token woman. Its first action was to register all retailers of foodstuffs. It then organised sugar cards for each household; these were to be completed and taken to the chosen retailer, who would stamp each half, retaining one and returning the other to the customer. The card had to be presented at the time of each weekly purchase of the ration.

Prices were also regulated: milk was to be sold at 6d per quart and potatoes at 1s per stone. The farmers' union quickly protested that these prices were artificially high. Another complaint was that the setting of maximum prices quickly meant that these became the norm. In December, turkeys, chickens and ducks were being sold at 3s the pound, about three times pre-war prices, while rabbits cost 2s and hares 7s each. Butter was priced at 2/6 per pound.

Meat was not yet rationed, and in this respect difficulties were foreseen with the wide variety of meats available, both fresh, pre-cooked (like ham and tongue) and tinned. As a prelude to rationing, householders were required to use their sugar cards to register with a butcher. This was an attempt to ensure fair distribution, and 'every effort is being made to ensure the provision of sufficient supplies'.

Heavy rain in August worsened the situation, with damage to the corn harvest, and potatoes rotting in the ground.

Again the *Observer* editor had his say on the matter:

'There is a real shortage of foodstuffs, which high wages and large incomes will not overcome. Thus it is the bounden duty of every householder – rich and poor alike – to economise, and to avoid waste as unpatriotic.'

The war reports were increasingly concerned with the torpedoing of merchant ships in the unrestricted submarine campaign which, in April 1917, brought the United States into the war. The political collapse of Russia was at the same time making her continued participation a matter of doubt.

On a lighter note there was the annual induction of the new High Sheriff of the County in May. The former Sir William Hesketh Lever, owner of the Sunlight soap factory and founder of the model village at Port Sunlight, was assuming office, hanging his shield in the Shire Hall. He took the opportunity to explain his new title, Lord Leverhulme, formed from his own surname and the maiden name of his late wife. He was to found a Lady Leverhulme Art Gallery, using a title which she had never in fact held.

On 4 August 1917, the anniversary of Britain's declaration of war, there was a mass open-air meeting outside the Town Hall. There a resolution was passed binding all to continue to support the war 'until it should be brought to a successful conclusion'. Since this coincided with the lack of success of the assault on the German lines in the Ypres area by British forces, the failure of the French offensive further south, and the imminent collapse of Russia, prospects for victory must have seemed remote.

A strike of engineers in the town was blamed by the *Observer* on the influence of *'German-made Socialism: the engineer in the shop is as much a combatant as the soldier at the front.'* Fortunately the issue was quickly settled when at a meeting the men concerned voted to return to work.

Payment for the war was increasingly a matter of concern. A national War Bonds scheme, with contributions as low as £5, had been started in 1915, and quickly raised £600 million, well in advance of its target. In January 1917 the council decided to invest £26,000 of its reserve fund in these five per cent bonds. In 1916 a National War Savings Week was held. Not only did this seek to raise money, but also to save in other respects – to buy nothing that was not essential, to cut down on food bills and food waste 'to meet the supreme needs of the nation'. Food prices were increasing, as supplies fell short as the German submarines took their toll of merchant shipping, and sugar reached 8d per pound.

As Christmas 1916 approached, the Mayoress asked for contributions to send Christmas parcels to the crew of HMS *Lancaster*, now flagship of the Pacific Squadron. 'Gifts of money, of navy blue mufflers and mittens, cakes, chocolates, cigarettes, tobacco and pipes' should reach the Town Hall by the end of November. The appeal was repeated, successfully the following year. At the same time the government announced a new organisation for sending parcels to prisoners of war, which superseded the system inaugurated by the Mayor in 1914. By the end of the year the King's Own had been authorised to form a Regimental Care Committee to collect and dispatch parcels. As there were almost 600 prisoners of war from this regiment alone, the running cost was estimated at £15,000 per year, and again the indefatigable Mayor headed an appeal for donations.

In 1916 the DORA instructions for action in case of an air raid were published. Although Lancaster was safe from naval or aerial bombardment, the town did experience destruction and death by the explosion at the White Lund munition works on 1 October 1917. The blast, which killed ten men, five of them firemen, was felt as far away as Burnley; shrapnel reached Quernmore and in Lancaster and Morecambe windows were blown in. The initial explosion happened in the evening, when most of the workers were at their supper break, saving heavier casualties.

Thomas Kew and Abraham Graham heroically shunted forty-nine ammunition trucks, loaded with 250,000 live shells out of the danger area, and both, together with Police Sergeant Thomas Coppard and works foreman Thomas Tattersall were awarded the Edward Medal, the highest award for courage shown by civilians. The rarity of this decoration is seen by the award of only twenty-five between its inception by King Edward VII in 1905 and its being subsumed into the George Cross in 1949.

For security reasons there was no direct report of the explosion in the press (although everyone in the neighbourhood must have been aware of it) other than an announcement from the Ministry of Munitions that an explosion had taken place 'in a factory in the north of England'. It was not until the announcement in June 1918 of the awards which had been made, that the citations revealed any detail. The medals for Graham and Kew were presented by the King a few days after the Armistice was signed.

Police Constable J. Johnson evacuated some 300 of the female workforce to safety, 'behaving with coolness and resource' while telephonist Mary Wilkinson cycled in from her home on the Marsh, was blown off her cycle in Cable Street as she reported for duty, but remained at her post for twenty-four hours 'rendering invaluable service at grave personal risk'. Both were later awarded the Medal of the Order of the British Empire, together with eleven other colleagues. These included John Caton, Alexander Chamberlain, William Disberry, William Heald, George Nutt and George Hutchinson (foreman), all of whom stayed at their posts in the Power House 'in spite of great danger'.

Nurses Lily Cope and Maisie Shepherd of the factory nursing staff had 'performed their duties quietly and without regard to personal safety'. Sergeant Richard Garth of the Lancaster Fire Brigade and Fireman Richard Taylor of the factory brigade both 'displayed great courage and resource on the occasion of a severe explosion at a national filling factory'. The other recipient of this medal was Foreman Charles Taylor who 'displayed great coolness and courage in carrying out vitally important repairs, whilst a number of shells were exploding in the immediate neighbourhood'.

Eight policemen – Fred Brocklehurst, William Hodgson, D'Arcy Moffat, Richard Newsham, George Oakes, Alonzo Savage, Daniel Sloan and William Wearing – were awarded the King's Police Medal. These awards were presented at a ceremony in the Ashton Hall by the Lord Lieutenant, Lord Shuttleworth. A guard of honour was provided by cadets of the OTC of the Royal Grammar School, and the band of the King's Own was in attendance.

The factory was out of commission for the rest of the war and many nearby houses were rendered uninhabitable. There had been an even more devastating, and much better-known explosion at Silvertown in

East London on 19 January in the same year, killing seventy-three, and even greater casualties at Faversham (105 deaths in 1916) and at Chilwell in 1918 where 137 were killed. The danger of the work to a largely female workforce was thus tragically underlined. A typical official announcement (for a different incident) read: 'The Press Bureau issued the following on Saturday. An explosion occurred this morning in a factory in the north of England, by which one person was killed and two injured. There was some damage to material.'

A new government regulation for workers in the munitions factories banned gambling. A case came before the court in November 1917, when seven employees pleaded guilty to playing Nap for pennies 'to while away the time'. As this was a first offence, they were only cautioned as to their contract, as a warning to others.

The dangers involved were highlighted by another fatal injury when Mr R.W. Rigg of Spring Garden Street was hit by a moving crane and died later of his injuries. At the inquest the Coroner recorded a verdict of accidental death, while a representative of the Ministry of Munitions expressed regret. Another death was recorded when a worker was using an emery wheel to polish the inside of a shell case. The wheel shattered and he died of multiple injuries, with the same verdict recorded.

The Munitions Court continued to hear cases of the breach of safety regulations, with two men each pleading guilty to having a pipe and matches in his possession. Both were sentenced to six weeks imprisonment with hard labour, on each of two counts. The commonest offences continued to be a refusal to work, absenteeism, neglecting work, talking and insubordination, but one employee was charged with 'being the worse for drink', and another with collecting for Dr Barnardo's Homes while on duty. One, charged with 'kissing a female employee' escaped punishment as she claimed that it 'had only been a bit of fun'.

The Chairman of the Tribunal was moved to comment that he would like to see some of the fit young men working in the munitions industry assigned to military service. He contended that some were using their work (with its high wages) as 'protection' and that others were misusing it by sleeping at work or playing cards. These, he felt, should lose their protected status.

At the start of 1917, a happier event was the provision by Mr Herbert Storey, of his customary New Year party for the elderly in the

Drill Hall. It was attended by 850 guests who were entertained by singers, instrumentalists and a ventriloquist. At this point the Grand Theatre was staging 'Little Red Riding Hood' twice nightly, described as 'an excellent entertainment, with speciality dances by eight dainty maids'. Not to be outdone, the Hippodrome featured the Radium Troupe of Dancers and the London Beauty Chorus in 'Find the Lady'. This was described as a 'Revusical musical comedy, an effective draw'. Large audiences paid between three pence and a shilling for their seats. At the Palladium one could see Edna Mayo and George Roby ('the Prime Minister of Mirth') in 'The Blindness of Virtue', with the added attraction of a three course lunch for 1/6 in the cinema's café, or a musical tea, entertained by Madame Ashworth's Savoy Trio. In November Dame Clara Butt gave another concert in the Ashton Hall, and a new act was that of the 'Ten Tommies' – discharged soldiers who gave 'a humorous entertainment with dramatic recitations'.

At a meeting of the Lancaster Trades and Labour Council the formation of a Labour Party for the Parliamentary division was announced. It expressed the hope that after the war there would be 400 Labour MPs out of a total of 702 members of the House of Commons. 'All the discontent arising from the war will aid them, and the passion for equality will be a powerful asset in their favour. The upper and middle classes are numerically inferior, and will be swamped in the flood of women and worker voters.'

At the same time a report of the Boundaries Commission proposed a wholesale revision of the Lancaster parliamentary division. Morecambe and Heysham would be transferred to the neighbouring Lonsdale division, while Fleetwood was to be added to Lancaster. This provoked great opposition both in Lancaster and Fleetwood, and the plan was withdrawn (though it has been implemented since).

A disappointing fall in the level of purchase of government War Bonds was reported in December. The initial response had been good, and bonds worth over £9,000 were bought in the first week in December, but the target was more than twice this amount. A War Bonds campaign was inaugurated by the Mayor, with the aim of raising £100,000, to build a submarine, the corporation subscribing £10,000, as did the Pearl Assurance Company. The sum of £90,000 was raised in the first four days, including amounts ranging from £5,000 from the Co-operative movement to £25 from Christ Church Infants' School,

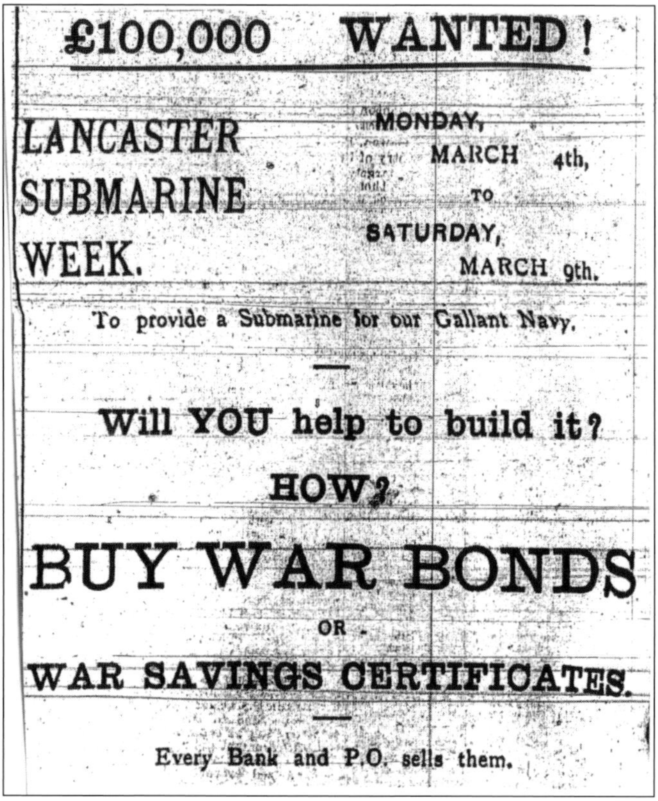

£100,000   WANTED !

LANCASTER
SUBMARINE
WEEK.

MONDAY,
MARCH 4th,
TO
SATURDAY,
MARCH 9th.

To provide a Submarine for our Gallant Navy.

Will YOU help to build it?

HOW?

BUY WAR BONDS

OR

WAR SAVINGS CERTIFICATES.

Every Bank and P.O. sells them.

and the target was met twice over. By the end of the war a total of £439,190 had been raised.

The Projectile Club celebrated New Year's Eve with a masked fancy dress ball, clearly a well-established favourite. The awards (all to women members) were to a cowgirl, a pierrette, a Spanish girl, a Dutch Boy and (appropriately for the pantomime season) a Prince Charming. Mr Storey's customary New Year party for the elderly opened 1918 held despite the constraints of food rationing. Once again over 850 attended, a fair proportion of them over 80. In Mr Storey's absence, the Mayor presided. The concert included the apparently obligatory ventriloquist.

The Grand Theatre was offering a 'musical comedy success' straight from the Shaftesbury Theatre, London, by the name of 'My Lady Frayler', while at the Palladium one might see 'The Village

Blacksmith', inspired by Longfellow's poem. Here, parents were urged not to miss giving children the opportunity to see the film 'Jackie in Wonderland'. This may have been occasioned by the stern warning that 'Where are My Children?' at the Picturedrome was for adults only. A 'special propaganda film', it dealt with the falling birth-rate, with admonitions to parents in its advertisement. 'Our boys should be told by their fathers the mysteries of sex and the dangers of ignorance. Girls should be told the same by their mothers, with the important warning that retribution falls so much more heavily on women than on men.' In the greatest possible contrast, the Hippodrome had a mixed programme of vocal and violin solos, dances by Madame Zillah's Gaiety Girls, and a pair of 'dialect comediennes'.

There were heavy falls of snow in January but, despite the weather and the war, the January sales were heavily advertised. Studholme's were offering 'exceptional bargains' in fur coats and fur muffs, at sale prices at their St Nicholas Street shop, with a special show of blouses and furs at Market Street. Their competitors, Manserghs were staging their '42nd Great Annual Sale', with a whole range of ladies clothes, dress materials and household items. The Co-operative stores offered ladies', children's and men's wear, while at Redmayne's a man might buy a suit for 35s. At Stewarts a suit cost 50s and an overcoat 35/6.

A presentation was made in February to Sir James McKechnie, managing director of Vickers of Barrow, which ran the projectiles factory. He had been awarded the KBE in the Honours List, and to mark this his employees presented him with a smoking cabinet, an illuminated address in the form of a book which also included their signatures – and a photograph of the millionth shell to come off the production line!

In February 1918 the passage of the Representation of the People Act was hailed by the editor of the *Observer* as

'One of the greatest reforms in modern history – the enfranchisement of six million young women [over 30, be it noted] and of a vast number of young men serving in the army and navy. It is as great a change as was brought about by the Great Reform Act of 1832, and greater than the extension of the franchise to householders in 1868, and to the agricultural labourers years later.'

The discrepancy between the male and female franchise was explained thus: *'if all women had voted on similar grounds to men, they would be able to swamp the latter, but as matters stand it is believed that males will still have the predominant voice, though in some towns women may outnumber the men.'*

A breakdown of the printing machine the following week delayed the production of the *Observer* until it could be run off on the machines of the *Guardian*.

The cinemas continued to operate and to advertise as usual. In June 1918 the Palladium was showing 'the World's Greatest Film – Intolerance', to be followed the next week by Mary Pickford as 'Rebecca of Sunnyside Farm', and later still would appear 'Griffith's Wonder Film – Birth of a Nation'. Patrons were reminded that 'the new electric 'buses stop and depart almost opposite our doors'. The establishment claimed to be 'The super cinema for all the big pictures, presenting a programme unsurpassed in or out of London', and an added bonus was the availability of Musical Teas in the Palladium Café. Seat prices ranged from 2d or 4d in the pit to 1s in the gallery, where advance booking could be made.

The Projectile Club continued to be as active as ever. A concert at the Club in June 1918 raised £54 for the Prisoners of War Fund, while a much more ambitious project later in the month was for a Grand Open Air Gala, to be held on the Giant Axe Field (if wet, in the club at the Collegian Rooms in Gage Street). A sports meeting and a cricket match were planned, with side shows and dancing to the National Projectile Factory Band, and refreshments provided by the factory's canteen staff. The weather was kind, but the sports meeting was cancelled, and the cricket match a short one, the two teams scoring only twenty-three runs between them.

At this time it would appear that the war had made hypochondriacs of the people of Lancaster – or at least that the advertisers hoped that it had. In a single issue of the *Guardian* in June, they offered Peps, to protect the chest, Formamint to heal a sore throat, Beecham's Pills for the digestive system and Doan's backache and kidney pills. Alternatively there was Veno's syrup for bronchial catarrh and Mrs Winslow's soothing syrup. Dr Williams's pink pills would cure debility, and of course there was always the inimitable Zam-Buk, now often advertised by means of testimonials from those who had found relief from this panacea.

TO ALL

HOME and COLONIAL

CUSTOMERS

RATIONING SCHEMES

You are free to register with your own Retailer.

Please remember that the Food Controller says :—

"Customers are urged to take their Cards to the Shopkeeper with whom they usually deal."

In the summer of 1918 came the imposition of overall food rationing, to take effect from 14 July. Ration books were to replace the existing cards for individual commodities, and application forms were distributed to each household, to be completed and returned to a centre in each ward – mainly the local schools. This would enable the distribution of the books – again by wards – by 13 July. Householders, as before, were to register with retailers but they were allowed to change their present registration at the outset of the scheme. At this time the need for an increase of home production of food was underlined by two poster appeals by the Ministry of National Service. The first was addressed to employers and local authorities. 'Can any of your men PLOUGH?', it enquired. 'There are thousands of men in civilian employment who understand ploughing. It is essential, in view of the grave menace to food supplies that these men should be released, wherever possible, for temporary work on the land. Lend these men to the state.'

The second was aimed at women: '10,000 women are required at once to grow and harvest the victory crops'. They were offered free outfits with high boots, breeches, overalls and hat, maintenance during training, travelling expenses and a wage of 18s a week (90p) for work on carefully selected farms.

Volunteers of a different kind were also sought: 'Five questions for women of today – can you do clerical work, cook, wait at table and do domestic work? If not, are you willing to try? Queen Mary's Army Auxiliary Corps needs 30,000 women immediately.'

The Care Committee for Prisoners of War continued to be very active, a report in 1918 showing 'the enormous amount of good work being accomplished in the dispatching of parcels of food and clothing to prisoners of the local regiment. To date over 2,500 parcels of food, and almost 4,000 of clothing had been sent, with total receipts of £17,000.'

In June of that year at the Grand Theatre over ninety performers (soloists, chorus and orchestra) gave an operatic programme in aid of the fund. The programme included excerpts from 'Rigoletto', 'Il Trovatore', 'Faust' and the lighter works 'Maritana', 'The Rose of Castille' and the 'Bohemian Girl'. The committee was able to record that during September 1917 the sum of almost £2,000 and in May 1918, £1,436 was raised, through a range of events including concerts, dances, jumble sales and collecting boxes in works, schools and cinemas. The fund-raising continued unchecked, with £6,000 being raised in the final three months of the war. By then over £450,000 worth of war bonds had also been bought in Lancaster.

A Lancaster branch of the National Association of Discharged Sailors and Soldiers was formed in mid-1917, and its first anniversary was marked by a procession led by the band of the King's Own, army and navy cadets, St John's Ambulance representatives and boy scouts. Numbers of the men followed, some on foot and some in charabancs. The Mayor, as ever, presided. In February 1918 the organisation was allowed the use of the Gregson Institute on Moor Lane by the vicar and council of Christ Church, whose parish hall it was. This gave the men rooms for social gatherings, a reading room and a billiards room.

America had joined the Allies in April 1917, as a result of the loss of their ships during Germany's unrestricted submarine campaign, but the country had a very small regular army, and it was well into 1918 before American troops arrived in Europe in any numbers. When it became known that trainloads of American soldiers had arrived at a northern port, and were to pass through Lancaster, great excitement was engendered, and crowds filled the platforms of the Castle Station to greet them. 'The people cheered, waved flags, sang patriotic songs and offered refreshments of tea, coffee, bread and butter and fruit.' Souvenirs were exchanged, including uniform buttons.

The fourth anniversary of Britain's entry into the war – 4 August – was celebrated as Remembrance Day, when the robed Mayor and Council processed to the Parish Church, preceded by the band of the King's Own, and followed by a parade of local volunteers, cadets and Girl Guides for a service. An open-air, non-denominational service was held in Market Square, organised by the Free Church Council.

In April 1918, the National Service authorities submitted a proposal to take over Dallas Road School. The Education Committee did not look favourably on this, but 'recognised that they must not stand in the way of a national department at this time'. Provisional arrangements were made, which consisted of the use of four classrooms in the Storey Institute for 180 girls, and five in the old Sulyard Street School for the same number of boys. The main room at High Street would cater for 120 younger pupils, with separate provision for 'mixed infants' under seven. The financial arrangements took some time, but by the end of the summer, all was ready.

A decision in December 1917 by the council to found a junior technical day school took effect in the summer of 1918, when the school was established in the Storey Institute, in the space vacated by the Girls' Grammar School on the opening of its new premises in 1914. The prospectus listed courses in applied sciences – in mechanical, electrical and chemical engineering, in draughtsmanship, and the building trade. There was provision for two-year courses to prepare boys of 13–15 for apprenticeships in these careers, as well as preparation for taking articles to architects and surveyors. A six-day week (with half days on Wednesdays and Saturdays) cost fees of 30s per year, payable in three termly instalments. Entrance tests were held on 24 July and the school opened on 9 September.

This represented a considerable step forward. Boys and girls were taught in the elementary schools up to the age of 13, but apart from those who were awarded scholarships to the grammar schools at 11 or those in private education, there was no provision for education beyond 13.

CHAPTER 9

The Coming of Peace

As the success of the Allied counter-offensive of the summer and autumn continued, it became clear that victory was only a short time away. An editorial in the *Guardian* looked towards peace and the challenges it would bring. The need to concentrate on the war had led to a cessation of building work, and there was 'a grievous lack of housing'. Thousands of disabled sailors and soldiers would continue to need the support of organisations like the Red Cross and St Dunstan's, which would in turn require financial support. Other immediate problems were grave shortages of water ('use every economy') and of coal for the approaching winter, while the question of the future government of Ireland, set aside for the duration of the war, would again become urgent.

The news of the signing of the Armistice was received during the morning of Monday 11 November, and 'in an incredibly short time the town was beflagged, public and private buildings being adorned'. The Mayor at once arranged a public demonstration in Dalton Square, and a fanfare by trumpets and cornets of the band of the King's Own was played here and at other locations. A service of thanksgiving was held at the Parish Church in the evening, and an open air service in Market Square was organised by the Free Churches.

The report in the *Observer* complimented the Mayor and Mayoress, *'who have had the felicity of leading the townspeople in public rejoicing. They have worked like Trojans in the hour of the town's need, they have done magnificently in providing comforts for local troops, and for all these things the town says thank you.* Mrs Briggs had already been honoured, along with three of her colleagues, by the King of the Belgians with the *Medaille de la Reine* for their work in the relief of Belgian refugees.

The vicar of Lancaster and Mrs Bardsley now encouraged the congregation to undertake the establishment of a new church to serve the Marsh, the result being the building of the little church of St George. There was also a proposal at this time for the division of the over-large diocese of Manchester, and the Ruri-decanal conference pressed for this to be based in Lancaster, as the ancient county town, with the beautiful parish church as the new cathedral, but the rival claims of Preston and Blackburn were also being canvassed, and eventually the choice fell on Blackburn.

The coalition government headed by Mr David Lloyd-George had already announced that a general election would take place soon after the end of the war. The editor of the *Observer* gave his opinion that *'Party divisions and party wrangles are quite out of place now. We cannot imagine that the people will withdraw support from the coalition government. To do so would weaken the country at the peace conference.'* There were, however, others who felt that the election should have been held over until peace was made.

A Representation of the People Act had widened the electorate to include all householders who were men over 21 or women over 30 (younger women would have to wait another ten years to gain equality in this respect). The Lancaster electoral register, published in July 1918 identified a total of 19,945 voters in the town (11,435 men and 7,710 women) though the total for the whole division was over 36,000. An open letter to the *Observer* from 'A Woman Voter' emphasised their new role in the political life of the country:

'We have done much towards the winning of the war, and the war has also done much for women. Such great progress has been made towards the realisation of our ambitions that we are naturally bewildered. The much-coveted vote is ours, and now there is to be the opportunity of using it, what use will the women of England make of the new privilege that they have given so much to ensure.'

Even before the Armistice, a meeting of the Lancaster Parliamentary

Division Unionist Association had adopted General Sir Archibald Hunter as its prospective candidate. General Hunter, late of the King's Own, had commanded the Aldershot depot during the war. The sitting member, Sir Norval Helme was adopted by his own Liberal Party Association, and supported by the Trade Union movement, but not by the coalition government, as he had voted against them on several occasions. Its support was instead given to General Hunter. There was a move to nominate a candidate to represent the interests of the Discharged Sailors and Soldiers Association, but this came to nothing, and the withdrawal of the prospective candidate for the Labour Party, Mr Joseph Binns, led to the local Co-operative movement declaring that it could not support either nominated candidate.

Sir Norval Helme campaigned mainly on his record as the sitting MP, but also pointed out that his opponent was a stranger to the district, with no experience of political matters, (though he had served as Governor of Gibraltar from 1910–1913), while General Hunter emphasised his backing from the coalition.

During the brief campaign, each held numerous meetings around the division, and each seemed to have substantial support. Polling was held on 14 December, but the announcement of the result was deferred for two weeks until the votes of soldiers could be counted. A total of 5,656 ballot papers had been sent to these men, of which 2,052 were returned. Out of a total electorate of almost 37,000, General Hunter secured 14,403 votes against 9,776 for Sir Norval, and was duly elected. He served only until 1922, when Sir Norval Helme was again elected.

CHAPTER 10

The Aftermath of War

Some soldiers were demobilised soon after the war ended, with the problems of reintegrating them into employment. A poster from the Ministry of Labour was published: 'He risked his life for you – are you going to give him a job? Go to your nearest Employment Exchange.'

Prisoners of war returned home (fifty to Lancaster during the first week in December). The *Observer* reported that *'good food, decent clothing and happy surroundings are working wonders with even the most emaciated and ill-looking men. They are all deeply grateful for the parcels of food and clothing sent them by the Care Committee, without which they say they could not have lived.'*

In January the Mayor and Mayoress hosted a welcome to repatriated prisoners of war at the Ashton Hall. It took the form of a 'smoking concert' to which each man was accompanied by a lady friend; there were entertainments, speeches and refreshments. A proposal for a Victory Ball was deferred until after Easter, when it passed off 'very enjoyably', with 250 tickets sold.

At a ceremony in the Parish Church in December, the colours of the 5th Battalion of the King's Own were returned from their war-time home in the Regimental Chapel, Captain N. Briggs, son of the Mayor and Mayoress, receiving them. (It is noteworthy that the church was then always referred to as the Parish Church rather than as the Priory and Parish Church, as now.) The 2nd Battalion of the King's Own returned from Mesopotamia in April 1919, marching to Bowerham Barracks, led by the regimental band.

HMS *Lancaster*, together with the other survivors of the County class of armoured cruisers, was decommissioned in 1919 and was sold to the shipbreaking firm of T.W. Ward, to be broken up at Preston (the firm also had a breaker's yard at the Stone Jetty at Morecambe). Her magnificent silver ship's bell is now in the city museum, and her white ensign, also presented by the mayor and corporation, was laid up in the Priory Church, where it still remains. There was a suggestion that a German submarine might be berthed at Glasson Dock, but Lancaster was instead promised a tank. There is no report that this ever materialised (the Germans had very few tanks) but a howitzer was awarded to the Royal Grammar School to mark the contribution of its former pupils to the war effort.

It had been resolved at a public meeting in November 1917 that there should be a memorial naming all the Lancaster men who gave their lives during the war. This is situated in a garden to the east of the Town Hall, with lawns, cherry trees and seating provided. It was dedicated on 3 October 1924, during the mayoralty of George Jackson, and bears the inscription 'In honoured memory of the men of Lancaster who gave their lives in the Great War 1914-18'. It is dominated by a large bronze figure of an angel representing Peace, and holding an olive

City war memorial (JWF)

City war memorial (JWF)

branch, with ten vertical panels listing the names of the dead. These, over a thousand in total, are listed alphabetically, with initials but without unit or rank.

Fifty pairs of brothers are identified, while five families lost three sons each, and one, the Butterworths, lost four. Their father had died in 1916 after the deaths of two of the sons: his doctor recorded 'a broken heart' as the cause of death. Mrs Butterworth was invited to participate in the dedication of the memorial, along with Mrs Gardner, Mrs Williams and Mrs Pritchett, each of whom had lost three sons. They unveiled the panels bearing the names of the dead.

Two more names from the first war are to be found on the adjacent memorial to those killed in the second war and later conflicts. It is still the focal point of Remembrance Day and Remembrance Sunday commemorations.

A well-attended public meeting in the Ashton Hall in late November 1918 pressed for a more practical memorial, in the form of homes for returning disabled soldiers. This had been presaged twelve months earlier, when Mr H.L. Storey had proposed an 'industrial village' in

Lancaster as a settlement for disabled servicemen of the King's Own; it would ensure them a home and employment on their return to civilian life. The resolution was seconded by the Reverend J.H. Shackleton Bailey, Headmaster of the Royal Grammar School, and supported by General Sir Archibald Hunter, Colonel of the Regiment. The *Observer* strongly supported the suggestion: *'Lancaster, already rich in public institutions for the benefit of the state, would be further enriched by this latest scheme.'*

Within months of the 1918 Armistice, a committee had been formed, issued a brochure requesting donations, and obtained charitable status for the project. Cottages, a hostel for the unmarried, workshops and social facilities were envisaged, on the West Field opposite Giant Axe, on land donated by the children of Herbert Storey.

Fund raising started immediately, with a performance of Handel's 'Messiah' among the first ventures, together with private and corporate donations. The final meeting of the Prisoners of War Care Committee, disposed of its remaining funds to various projects, with £1,000 donated to the Royal Lancaster Infirmary and £2,500 to the Westfield

Westfield House, administrative office of the village (JWF)

Bowling Green (JWF)

Cottage at the village (JWF)

Village. Although government funding was
refused and opposition from the trades unions
caused the closure of the workshops, the houses,
a social club and a bowling green were created.
Westfield Memorial Village was opened in
November 1924, by Field Marshal Earl Haig.
Later, the focal point, a statue of a soldier giving
water to a wounded comrade, was unveiled by
General Sir Archibald Hunter.

There are wide lawns, trees and flower beds,
and the cottages each bear plaques naming
battles, individual soldiers or fundraisers,
number one appropriately bearing the name of
Herbert Storey. ('Cottage' is a distinctively

Statue of the soldier

Lancaster misnomer – most were substantial semi-detached houses,
though there were some bungalows.) The main street is Storey Avenue
and there is a Peel Crescent and a Haig Avenue. Individual cottages are
named for Western Front battles, such as Marne, Ypres, Le Cateau, but
also Gallipoli and Mesopotamia, where the second battalion of the
King's Own fought. Others are named for King's Own winners of the
Victoria Cross, or for individual soldiers where the families had made
specific donations, or to the 'Old Pals' and the Co-operative stores.

A handsome memorial at Bowerham School is framed in oak (by
Gillows) and bears the names, first of the eighty-eight killed in the war,
and then of 578 who served. These last included six names in blue, of
women who had been pupils at the school, but their role has not been
recorded. The decorations are also recorded, with one VC, four
Distinguished Conduct medals, three Military Crosses and seven
Military Medals. The panels are flanked by allegorical figures. A fine
Book of Remembrance, given by the Lancaster Military Heritage
Group records the service details of those who fell.

At Lancaster Royal Grammar School, the Old Lancastrian Club
lobbied for a war memorial in the planned New Building, and it was
opened in 1929. It is a handsome room, with linenfold panelling (by
Gillows) and matching bookcases. A plaque records the names of
seventy-five former pupils of the school who died in the war. These
are a microcosm of the national figures in that the majority of the deaths
were in actions on the Western Front including one on the first day of

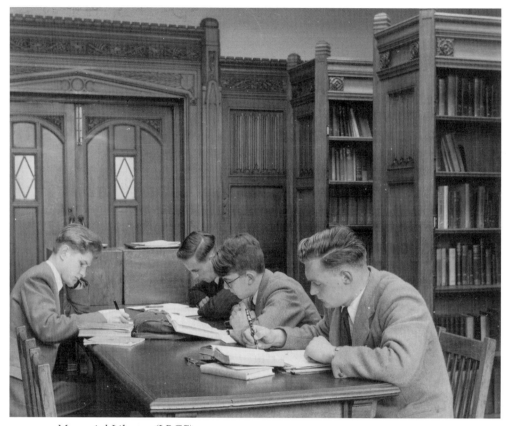

Memorial Library (LRGS)

the Battle of the Somme in 1916. Others fell at Gallipoli, in Mesopotamia, German East Africa and at sea. The donations also permitted the purchase of the memorial playing fields on Derwent Road.

Other memorials were set up in Waring & Gillows, the Co-operative store, the Castle station, the churches and schools, and the Post Office – about thirty in all. In 1915 a Roll of Honour was set up in Storey's White Cross mill, listing some 300 employees already serving in the army. Of these, 206 were with the King's Own, twenty-seven with 10 Battery Royal Field Artillery and sixty-four scattered among fourteen other army units. A photograph was featured in each local newspaper, but the original appears to have been lost.

These have all been catalogued by the Lancaster Military Heritage Group, with details and photographs. Some have been moved to new locations because of the closure of their original locations. Memorials from the four Methodist churches are now all in the remaining church at Greaves; that from the Gillows building is now in the Town Hall. St John's Church houses, as well as its own memorials, those from St Anne's (now the Duke's Theatre) and Bulk. The Priory is the location of the King's Own Chapel and the memorials of 10 Battery Royal Field Artillery and the St John's Ambulance Brigade.

The Church of Scotforth Saint Paul has no formal memorial, but a file naming eighty-three members of the parish who fell has recently been opened, the names provided by the Lancaster Military Heritage Group. They display the accustomed diversity of unit, rank and theatre of war. Among the names we find those of James Blackburn of Wellington Road, a private in the King's Own who died at Kut-el-Amara in Mesopotamia in April 1916 and Corporal John Bland of Graham Street, serving with the Cheshire Regiment, killed in Serbia in September 1918. Second Lieutenant James Gorst of Rosebery Avenue was in the Royal Field Artillery and fell in France on 29 May 1917, while Captain Charles Allen Hinton (Royal Engineers) had won the MC and bar before his death in May 1918. Private E. Wilcock of the Royal Marine Light Infantry died in 1917 in France and Sergeant L. Williams of the King's (Liverpool Regiment) was killed at Khartoum in the Sudan in 1916.

The first weeks of 1919 again brought heavy snow, with the result that road traffic was impeded, trains were delayed and telephone and telegraphic communications were interrupted. The waterlogged fields hampered farm work, but at least the reservoirs were filled, ending the water crisis. The employment exchange at the old Town Hall was at full capacity to cope with the demobilised soldiers, working until 10pm, including Saturdays. And this would only be the start – until the peace treaties were signed, an army had to be kept in the field, with only those men seen as key workers in their trades being demobilised early.

Production ceased at the National Projectile factory, with many women being transferred back to their home towns and local men resuming work where they had formerly been employed, before being directed to the factory by the tribunals. The council tried to get the

Market Stalls and Liptons Grocery (LCM)

Ministry of Munitions to continue to employ some discharged sailors and soldiers in the works, which was in use as a warehouse, with facilities for storage and the repair of machinery; there was a meeting at the Hippodrome to press the case. A major sale of 700 lots of machine tools attracted representatives from over 500 engineering firms across the country. Bidding was brisk, with over £150,000 realised, but it represented the death knell for the works.

One side effect was the availability of the YWCA hostel in China Street, which had opened to house some of the women coming from other towns, to be available as a social centre for local girls, with an initial membership of 200. It opened with a fancy dress ball, but as this was for members only, the girls had to accept their friends dressed in male costume as their partners.

There was a well-attended meeting in the Friends' Meeting House for a lecture on the League of Nations. The formation of such a body had been one of President Woodrow Wilson's Fourteen Points for peace. The Cambridge lecturer said that the League was vital to the preservation of peace, but that European statesmen blew 'hot and cold' about it, expressing great reservations. He contrasted the views of the French Premier and the American President, not of course knowing that while France would become one of the permanent members of the League Council, the American Senate would prevent US participation.

In the 17 January issues of the local papers the full details of the explosion at the White Lund shell filling factory were published. These have featured in Chapter 8, but what was now revealed for the first time was the extent of rumours of later casualties. Two weeks after the original disaster, a shell had exploded during the clearing-up of the debris, killing two men. Their inquest details were now published, putting to rest the rumours of a hundred further casualties, buried in an unmarked mass grave.

In May there was a council bye-election in Castle Ward, caused by the elevation of Councillor Seward as Alderman after the death of Alderman Heald. Mrs Anne Helme put herself forward as a candidate, and was duly elected as the first woman councillor in 700 years. She had already been very active in municipal affairs, serving on the Education Committee, as a member of the Board of Guardians, and as a governor of the Girls' Grammar School. She had been 'war secretary' to the Mayoress, and was currently an active supporter of the Westfield

Memorial Village. She was welcomed by the Mayor and Council as a colleague – but as Mrs Walter Croft Helme. (Her husband had died some years before, but this was then the formal way to address a widow.) Again the editor had his say, this time free from the vaguely patronising air which had marked his earlier comments on women:

> *'Ladies of Mrs Helme's temperament and training may bring a new note into public affairs. There is scope for women with vision and sagacity, and it is possible that the presence of ladies on town councils may raise the tone and outlook.'*

She later (in 1932–3) became Lancaster's first woman mayor. In May too there came the end of food rationing and the associated coupons, but the progress of the peace negotiations at Versailles was slow, the German delegates raising all kinds of objections and counter-claims when they were summoned to hear the Allies' demands. The Council proposed that celebrations of a Peace Day should be pre-arranged in advance, but that the celebrations should be delayed until the treaty was actually signed. There were impromptu festivities when the news broke that the Germans were about to sign. Rumours seemed to be validated when the 'calling bell' of the parish church was rung. The crowds quickly gathered in the town centre and flags appeared on the Town Hall and on other public and private buildings. There were fireworks, and the burning of effigies of the now ex-Kaiser.

PEACE was the headline on Friday 27 June, with the formal celebrations deferred until 19 July. These began with the ringing of the church bells of St Mary's, St Peter's and St Thomas's from 9am for an hour, followed by a thanksgiving service outside the Town Hall. All 8,000 schoolchildren in Lancaster were given a commemorative medal with the arms of the borough, and a sixpence (riches for a child in 1919). In the afternoon there was a children's party on Giant Axe Field (organised by the William Smith Easter Festival Committee) with sports, including not only conventional events, but sack and three-legged races, with over 3,000 entrants. There followed entertainments including Morris dancing and performing dogs and two bands were in attendance.

A procession from Haverbreaks to Skerton had tableaux representing the part played by the town in the war. Two floats showed the work of the National Projectile Factory and the shell-filling plant, two more the work of Waring and Gillows in making aircraft wings, ammunition boxes and other hardware. Ex-servicemen and women, the St John's Ambulance Brigade, VAD nurses the Women's Land Army, the Prisoner's Care Committee, cadets, scouts, and guides all took part. The evening was illuminated by Admiralty flares, there were fireworks and bands played for the dancing. The council had voted the sum of £780 to cover the expenses, and 'the merriment kept up until a late hour'.

The following weeks saw a succession of unofficial local celebrations – street parties, processions and sports being held in various areas of the town, with bands and dancing. There was a civic reception to welcome back the 6th Battalion of the King's Own, on its return from service in Mesopotamia, with crowds assembling in Dalton Square. Garden parties for all ex-servicemen and their wives or lady friends were planned for August, but in view of the unreliable nature of Lancaster's weather these were postponed until the last week in October and were held in the Town Hall. Over 1,000 guests attended on each of nine successive nights and all were welcomed at the top of the main staircase by the Mayor and Mrs Briggs.

This was their last public duty. At the next council meeting he was to be succeeded by Councillor G. Wright, but first a silver rosebowl and an illuminated address were presented to 'the Mayor who has held office during the most stirring period of Lancaster's modern history. He and Mrs Briggs have risen to every new demand that the exigencies of the troublous times has made. They have never faltered, never grown weary, but have served the town whole-heartedly. They have braved all the storms, overcome all the difficulties and have been equally successful in dealing with the problems of peace as well as of war.'

The councillors later elected him to fill the next Aldermanic vacancy, and portraits of both of them hang in the Mayor's Parlour at the Town Hall.

Following the celebrations, Lancaster had to face the future. Soldiers were being demobilised now in large numbers, and would be hoping to resume their pre-war work. Some were to face difficulties: one disabled ex-soldier was told by an employer that 'it was not his policy to employ cripples'. The staple industries of the town would gradually get back to their pre-war levels of staffing and production and, in the case of Gillows, to abandon their wartime production of war materials. The council had already begun to address itself to humdrum but necessary work, such as the widening of Cheapside and the repair of Scotforth Road and East Road. The overhaul of the electrical department was a priority, with an out-of-date plant being expensive to run.

Probably the major decision was to build council housing to support the government's pledge for 'homes for heroes to live in'. Much accommodation in the town centre was quite inadequate, lacking what were now considered to be basic amenities such as hot and cold running water and indoor toilets. The Greaves nurseries covered 45 acres of land between Scotforth and Bowerham Road, with easy connection to the tramway services as well as to sewage, gas and water mains. An initial plan for 400 new homes was later increased to 750, with land on the Marsh also being used.

The *Lancaster Observer* commented at the time of the publication of an Honours List:

> '*It is a wonder that the Mayor has not received any acknowledgement of his devoted service. Few mayors can have given so much time and done such good work as Mr and Mrs Briggs. Lancaster people know what they have done and appreciate it. They have not spared themselves in any way – they have given time, money and business ability to a multitude of causes. Few have worked harder, or even as hard, as the Mayor who has given himself entirely to public work. Lancaster people would have been glad to have seen Mr and Mrs Briggs included in the Honours List.*'

Sources

The *Lancaster Guardian* and the *Lancaster Observer* from 1914
  onwards.
A History of Westfield Memorial Village by Martin Purdy
Lancaster City Museum archives
Lancaster Military Heritage Group website

Photographs

Most of the photographs in this book have been provided by Lancaster City Museum, and are designated (LCM). Three from Lancaster Royal Grammar School are marked (LRGS), while my own are shown with my initials.

Index